ADULT LEARNERS

(A Research Study)

Theodore E. Andrews • *W. Robert Houston* • *Brenda L. Bryant*

Developed by Teacher Corps

Published, Washington, D.C. – 1981, by
ASSOCIATION OF TEACHER EDUCATORS

Association of Teacher Education
1900 Association Drive
Reston, Virginia 22091

This material was produced pursuant to Contract Number 300-77-0156 between the Center for Urban Education at the University of Nebraska at Omaha and the Teacher Corps, United States Office of Education, Department of Health, Education and Welfare. Contractors undertaking projects under such government sponsorship are encouraged to freely express their professional judgment in the conduct of such projects. Points of view or opinion stated here, therefore, do not represent official positions or policy of the United States Office of Education.

Development Training Activities Contract Director:
Floyd T. Waterman

Adult Learners was published by the Association of Teacher Educators. All manuscripts are reviewed by members of the Communications Committee. Points of view and opinions are those of the individual authors and not necessarily those of the Association.

TABLE OF CONTENTS

FOREWORD

In 1979, ATE was pleased to publish *Designing Short-Term Learning Experiences*, a volume that was both timely and well done. Now we are again pleased to offer to our members a companion publication, *Adult Learners*.

Both volumes report on studies of Teacher Corps sponsored workshops, the Corpsmember Training Institute (CMTI). However, they address issues and findings far broader than these institutes. In the first volume, the authors drew upon their experiences to make recommendations to people planning institute/workshops. In this volume, the authors address the problems of planning learning programs for adults. Specific recommendations are made, a detailed research study is reported, and suggestions for future steps are given.

We feel this study is particularly timely as increasing attention is being addressed nationally on the "adult learner." The research reporting a study of 400 adults in a three-week structured learning program utilizing pre- and posttest scores and daily observations is a major contribution to the study of adults.

ATE believes all educators will find this volume helpful and interesting.

Robert J. Stevenson
Executive Director
Association of Teacher Educators

ACKNOWLEDGEMENT

The research reported herein was conducted in conjunction with Teacher Corps Corpsmember Training Institute held during July 1979 in San Diego, California. The scope of the data collection and the demands placed on instructors and institute directors were great. It is to their tolerance and cooperative support that this report is dedicated. At every decision point, superb assistance and rigorous adherence to the study specifications were encouraged.

While it would be virtually impossible to identify everyone who made this study possible, several persons require special mention. Floyd Waterman, Instructional Leader for the Institute as well as the Director responsible for its operation, provided both conceptual and administrative support. James Steffensen, Associate Director, Development Branch, Teacher Corps, asked the right questions and supported efforts for rigor in the study. William Smith, Director, Teacher Corps, during this study, provided vision and leadership, while Paul Collins and Beryl Nelson ironed out more than one troublesome area.

Cynthia Rodriquez, Norma French, Richard Andrews, and Laura Andrews served as primary data collectors. They monitored the administration of the posttest achievement test and completed observations in each of the clusters. Throughout CMTI, each strived for validity and reliability in observations.

Each of the ten clusters had a team of three faculty, led by a cluster leader. These were free to design and organize instruction within certain predetermined constraints. Each team projected its own approach and instructional values as faculty worked with about forty participants. Instructional teams gave generously of their time and opened their clusters willingly to testing and observations. The clusters leaders were Tony Archuleta, Michael Barry, Brenda Bryant, Jack Croghan, Marcia Galli, Bill Moore, Carlos Olivarez, Daisy Reed, Julia Roberts, and Wallace Woodard.

Also, Robert S. Soar and Donald M. Medley assisted us in the design and analysis of the data. We are particularly appreciative of their efforts.

Finally to the 400 participants who completed pretests prior to coming to CMTI, posttests at the end of the institute, and interacted formally and informally with the study team, we are grateful.

In undertaking this study we hope that we have been both introspective and reflective. Brenda Bryant, one of the co-authors of this report, was also a cluster leader at CMTI. She did not participate in the design of the study, nor in the analysis of the data. She did, however, complete the Review of Related Research and, more importantly, wrote the "Epilogue" at the conclusion of this report. Her reactions and suggestions are both personal and professional. Her experience in designing evaluation studies is extensive, as is her professional interest in adult learning. As she indicates, she clearly is a participant observer. Too seldom have research studies included this added perspective. She raises a number of significant issues that we and our readers may wish to address in the future.

WRH
TEA
BLB

ADULT LEARNERS

(A Research Study)

INTRODUCTION

- *Floyd T. Waterman*

This volume and the research conditions from which the data are drawn are rather unique and should make a significant contribution to the field of education of adult learners. As Andrews points out in Chapter I, the population of adult learners is ever increasing, leading to the assumption that America, more than any other nation, has a broader range of learning activities in its schools, industry, business, and in its general population. The findings of this study are of interest to program designers who aspire to work successfully with adult learners.

It is my pleasure to have been associated with the authors of this volume over a span of more than a decade, although I have worked most closely with all three of them in the context of this study during the last five years. The experiences with the Teacher Corps programs have a much broader application to education than most observers acknowledge at first glance. The target population is comparable (in age and educational level) to that of most inservice activities of schools. Moreover, these Teacher Corps experiences provide a database research observation under conditions seldom experienced in educational programs. I am proud of my personal role in providing the laboratory for these researchers to study adult learning and feel good about the results of their efforts.

The Corpsmember Training Institute (CMTI), the educational setting for this study, is a rather unique learning environment. Andrews provides an excellent description of the CMTI in Chapter II, but I would like to suggest that many of our learning activities embodied the best practices that are suggested by the data in this research. We placed learners in situations in which there was teaming for learning as well as teaming by instructors; we provided simulations and opportunities for active involvement beyond the lecture-t type experience; and we encouraged instructors to personalize the material for the CMTI participants. Operating as a temporary system, the CMTI provided a rich resource of materials and techniques to instructors, involved instructors in planning, then provided considerable autonomy within the cluster for the three instructors to meet the objectives of the institute. While the constraints of the funding agency demanded a fairly cognitive program, the actual research data show that instructors who elected to do so could provide the type of learning environment that fostered both personal and cognitive gains. Learning occurred in all of the clusters, but it was no surprise that those clusters which had the greatest gains were those in which there was substantial stress on the affective and interactive processes. Let us proceed with an introduction to each of the chapters in the monograph.

Chapter I by Andrews contends that adult learning as a field lacks a conceptual model as the basis for developing and designing better programs for adults. He mentions as a factor to consider differences in personality in adults. Furthermore, adults experience physical changes which may appear slow in contrast with the changes taking place in children or adolescents, but which do affect the learning process. Adults are prone to be less "test wise" than youth and adult learners are likely to have an increase in dogmatism and rigidity after age 65. However, it is encouraging to note that the well-conditioned mind has no predetermined limits.

Andrews, early-on in the chapter, suggests that most adult training programs are NOT designed for adults; rather, they are developed by instructors who use what they have experienced regarding the teaching of children, adolescents, or perhaps college students. The key point is that while many of the accepted learning principles are valid for adults, differences in personality and learning styles do exist, and program designers should take cognizance of those differences and incorporate them in new designs.

The authors of this volume have reported some design principles worthy of noting and using in mounting adult learning programs. These are:

- Pay attention to the individual learner
- Pay attention to the affective as well as the cognitive domains
- Teach self-awareness as well as reflective learning skills
- Value the life experiences of the learners
- Provide alternative ways of doing things
- Support self-centered learning
- Be aware that repeated teaching of cognitive material will NOT necessarily lead to greater achievement.

As the person responsible for planning and mounting the adult learning programs upon which this research is based, I am not unmindful of the difficulties one encounters in an attempt to find out as much as possible about the learners before designing the program. My colleagues and I also operated under certain constraints of the funding agency: The Teacher Corps, whose national director called for a "rigorous learning environment" typical of graduate schools. Such programs often reflect a high standard of instruction which is expected of programs designed primarily around the desire to disseminate highly cognitive material all too often presented in an unproductive manner. Note the design features that grow out of the work of the authors of this volume. The principles to which they subscribe, and which should be added to the list above, undergird the activities that Andrews recommends for instructors of adults to help personalize learning:

- When adults are more personally and actively involved in the learning situation, they learn more cognitive material.
- As people become more mature, they are less alike with respect to conditions under which they learn.
- Adults who do not perceive a need for or have a desire to learn, *won't learn*.
- An instructor of adults must understand what motivates his or her students.

Chapter I closes with three exhibits that should be useful to those designing instructional programs for adults: (a) skills of moderators; (b) content for learning; and (c) the learning process.

In Chapter II, Andrews provides a history of the three previous institutes which made up the background and experience of the authors and describes how the studies were developed. The fourth CMTI, held in 1979, was the basis for the present research study. The CMTI was truly a living-learning laboratory and the presence of the data gatherers and researchers added an additional benefit to the CMTI. All of the conclusions regarding the adult learning were data-based and were veritifications of findings from previous institutes conducted under very similar circumstances. Of the four institutes described, the 1979 was probably the best organized in terms of the content areas and available materials because it was based upon a backlog of previous experience. Demographic data on the subjects of the study are summarized in tables provided at the close of the chapter.

Brenda Bryant held a unique position in this study. In the previous CMTIs she was involved as a researcher and evaluator, but in the 1979 study, she was a cluster leader and had both design and instructional duties. Thus, she did not participate in the gathering of data for this study, but had an opportunity to work with Andrews and Houston to review research, and to write a personal reaction to it. In Chapter III, she acts as a reviewer of research and offers a summary and conclusions on teacher effectiveness, time-on-task and attending behaviors, teacher moves and methods, and student characteristics.

While most of the research on teacher effectiveness relates to elementary students, Bryant points out that such studies have begun to add to our knowledge about the techniques of questioning and classroom management. These studies also speak of issues related to classroom management, class size, and grouping. Teacher characteristics regarding directness, praise, feedback, student involvement, teacher attitudes and classroom climate are also reviewed.

Findings relative to time-on-task suggest that time engaged is related to achievement in the basic skills, mostly in elementary grades; yet there is a gap insofar as students from various backgrounds and involvement in various subjects is concerned. She concludes that one virtually ignored area is that of time-on-task with adult populations. The present study contributes to the body of knowledge in that area.

"Inconclusive" and "contradictory" are terms Bryant uses to describe the research on teaching methods. Lecturing and discussion methods have been studied, mostly with secondary students, and although there are variations (depending upon content studies), both methods appear to be effective. Less thoroughly studied, however, are "experimental methods" though available data suggests that "this method is about as effective as those to which it has been compared". Researchers in several studies conclude that a somewhat structured approach to teaching is most effective and that methods do vary in efficiency and in effect on student attitudes.

The characteristics of elementary students have been described in greater detail than is the case for adult learners. Factors such as socio-economic status, cultural background, subject matter studied, and learning styles all seem to influence student learning.

Adult learning researchers and theorists agree that adults differ from one another in needs, styles, strategies, and preferences. However, there is agreement among most adult educators that adults require self-directed, self-paced learning that is relevant to their personal or vocational interests. This is particularly so for the most mature learners. Adults expect to rely on their experiences and abilities as they engage in learning activities and seem to prefer process approaches rather than content approaches. Adults like to have the educator provide the structure while they as learners engage in study for themselves. Effective use of time, accuracy, and mastery of content are also important to adults.

The reader will find Chapter III especially helpful in that it provides a carefully selected and focused bibliography of readings related to teaching methods, student characteristics, and time-on-task research.

In Chapter IV, Houston provides the background, statement of problems, and procedures used in the present study in the areas of time-on-task and complexity of concepts. The problem for this research study is defined as:

What is the relationship between instructional time and adult achievement, taking into consideration differences in content, complexity of concepts and methods of instruction?

The three content areas for the institute studies were the study of organizations, multicultural education concepts, and community-based education. As Houston says, the first area was considered as primarily cognitive in content, while the other two involved cultural and personal affective overtones. Using Bloom's definitions, achievement was defined with reference to the complexity of concepts. Specifically, these concepts were the dichotomous analysis of lower cognitive concepts, knowledge and comprehension, and higher cognitive concepts such as analysis, synthesis, and application.

Extensiveness of instructional time was defined as the *observed* instructional time devoted to the three subject areas. Instructional methods were also analyzed. Types of instruction (in each of the content areas) were classified as:

• presentation of low cognitive content
• presentation of high cognitive content
• discussion
• experimental processes concerned with cognition

Two other instructional methods were studied that were not specifically related to one of the three content areas. These were: experimental, non-cognitive processes, and non-instructional activities. The fourteen methods of instruction (four for each of the three content areas, plus two general methods) were considered both in logical combinations and individually.

Houston describes the achievement tests developed, their validity testing, collection of the data from the 400 participants, and the analysis of the data. He also describes the procedures for observers collecting data on instructional times.

It was found that organizational theory and multicultural education concepts were the basis for instruction to a greater extent than community-based concepts (33.30% and 35.54% compared to 13.66%). Presentations, discussions, and experimental activities related to the three content areas accounted for 82.50% of the time, but 47.62% of that time was devoted to presentations. These were not necessarily lectures, but the majority of these presentations were concerned with high-cognitive concepts (37.74%) and 9.88% to low-cognitive-based presentations. During one-fifth of the time, discussions were conducted. It was found that high achieving clusters spent more time in presentations and in experimental activities and less time in non-instructional activities.

In Chapter V, Houston explores the second problem: Were any differences in attitude among clusters related to achievement in those clusters and was there a relationship between (a) achievement and (b) attitude and personal characteristics among individual participants? Data were gathered from pre- and posttest achievement scores of individual participants; personal characteristics and attitude toward the institute were elicited as part of the posttest. Participants expressed highest ratings for the faculty with general attitude toward the CMTI as second.

When dealing with the question: "Were there any differences in attitude among clusters related to achievement in those clusters?", it was concluded that there was no relation between achievement and attitude. Three findings emerged:

1. Persons with a positive attitude toward a content area tended to obtain higher achievement in that area.
2. The higher the grade level (of teaching) preferred, the greater achievement scores in highly cognitively oriented content.
3. Years of teaching experience was positively related to achievement in high cognitive concepts.

Chapter VI presents conclusions and implications by Houston and Andrews. Houston and Andrews point to the need for comprehensive studies of adult motivation, learning styles, appropriate instructional modes for adults, and other applied research. This research study provides some insights that would be helpful to persons designing adult education programs: the problems of time devoted to instruction and achievement and the problem of exploring the relationship of participant attitudes and personal characteristics to adult achievement.

Instructional time was examined in 50 twenty-minute observations of ten clusters. The relationship between time devoted to instruction and achievement was weak but positive. In the second problem, 27 items were related to nine scales. It was found that the instructional areas that included the strongest affective components were most highly prized. However, there were no significant differences between cluster mean achievement and participant attitude.

Houston and Andrews comment that adults may be less influenced by time variables than children or youth because of the varied efficiency of their individual learning styles, different motivation for understanding particular topics, increased maturation, a wide range of learning modes not related to time, and greater familiarity with concepts being taught. Because adult learning occurs in such a complex content, isolation of the effects of time is more difficult. Houston and Andrews then suggest that the study raised more questions than it answered and discuss problems related to the inability to control learning modes or individuals. Despite these issues, it is my feeling that those involved in adult education program design will gain much from the new insights related to cautions suggested in the research: (1) designers need to involve the participants; (2) there is a need to personalize instructions; and (3) the designer of adult education programs must re-think assumptions about adult learners. There is a great need to recognize the uniqueness of adults as learners and the differences in their motivation as compared with youth and children.

If learning is to be a life-long adventure, designers must provide adult learners with opportunities for a greater involvement in the decisions about learning.

In Chapter VII, an epilogue by Bryant, there are comments regarding the theoretical framework of studies on adult learning, comments about evaluation design and methodology, and study populations.

It is a sensitive, thoughtful essay which should be a useful guide to future researchers. Four questions are worthy of focus at this point:

- To what extent are adult learners setting their own objectives and working toward their achievement?
- To what extent are learners engaged in self-evaluation?
- To what extent are learners a resource to one another?
- To what extent is the learner able to describe how the learning will be applied in other settings?

What she suggests is that researchers as well as program designers should attempt to guide their work by insights and principles of adult learning. She calls for possible use of action research rather than carefully controlled research as a possible way to involve and to educate future teachers. She also suggests that we need more information and better definitions of "adult" before we proceed to examine adult learning. She also suggests that other variables such as the living-learning environment, the dynamics of instructor perception, individual learners, and purposes are important. She concludes her comments with the remark that she has perhaps raised more questions than answered.

A Personal Perspective

As one involved in the planning, operation, and administration of the four institutes, it is clear to me that I cannot completely remove myself from a personal involvement, but I feel this volume will be helpful to staff development designers as they attempt to design programs for adult learners. Certainly I can endorse the rigor with which Andrews and Houston undertook the research, yet I am sympathetic to the "action-research" approach suggested by Bryant. It is true that results may have been more pronounced had it been possible to focus on the individuals more than the class (or clusters) involved in the study. But the reader is reminded that these data are based upon observations that were carefully controlled rather than upon self-reporting by instructors, as is often the case with studies dealing with methodology and time-on-task. The effort is a good beginning that gives us some new insights which should be useful to program designers and to that end this volume is dedicated. I commend my colleagues for their effort and recommend it highly to the reader.

Chapter 1

IMPROVING ADULT LEARNING PROGRAMS

- *Theodore E. Andrews*

The number of learning programs for adults is increasing rapidly. The range of such efforts appears endless: adult basic education offerings, training programs given by corporations, professional inservice programs, the vast efforts of the human potential movement, personal interest offerings, etc. The list goes on and on. Adults participate in such programs for many different reasons: to secure a job, to achieve a diploma or a degree, to gain a promotion, to improve their lives, and possibly, as with mountains, simply because they are there.

Despite the popularity of these efforts, there is considerable criticism about many of these programs. In particular, inservice education programs often are criticized for their irrelevance to the real needs of teachers. Certainly many improvements in such programs have occurred in the past few years, but the criticisms do not stop. We, in this publication, are suggesting one major reason why these criticisms continue.

Educational programs are not designed for adults. They are designed primarily by instructors who use what they have learned (or more likely have experienced) about teaching children, adolescents, or college students. While many of the principles of learning are the same for adults and children,

*differences do exist, and only by careful attention to those
differences will consistently successful learning programs for
adults be offered.*

A variety of ideas, theories, and assumptions exist about
how adults learn. What does not exist is a conceptual approach
to adult learning which brings together what is known about
adults as learners, theories on adult development, and research on adult learning. With a conceptual model one can
begin to design programs for adults. In this publication, we
are presenting the basis for such a model.

Adults as Learners

Some educators believe that there are no differences in
how adults and children learn. We believe that there are and
that it is necessary to look at the similarities as well as the differences.

James E. Birren defines learning as "a relatively lasting
modification of behavior as a result of experience." He also
believes that there are three aspects to a learning experience:
the experience must be registered, retained and recalled
(Birren, 1964). Certainly, this definition is as applicable for
youth as it is for adults. We believe the differences exist not
because of the definition of learning, but rather because of
differences in personality. There are three components of
personality: biological drives, behavior control, and personal
standards (Birren, 1964). "All three appear to change with
age: our food and sexual wants diminish, our concept of reality changes, and our ideals and standards, though relatively
stable, keep evolving over the life span (Zinberg & Kaufman,
1963)." It is these changes that persist over time that make
adult learners different from learners who are young. Certainly youth go through changes (some even very pronounced),
but these changes are often tied directly to a young person's
growth. These changes are rapid and compressed into short
periods of time.

The physical changes in an adult for the most part are
slow and almost imperceptible. Decades blend together and
the excitement and memories of one's "first experiences"

become blurred by repetitions of similar occurrences. The adult often will experience little change for years; yet only to have change occur unexpectedly with frightening impact due to outside circumstances such as death, illness, divorce, etc.

Research on aging also supports the fact that there are differences. Studies have shown that older adults score more poorly than younger people on tests of critical thinking. An analysis of the data reveals that the older adults show less objectivity in answering certain questions and a general sense of inflexibility in their responses (Birren, 1964). Another study reveals that after age 55 adults show an increase in rigidity and dogmatism (Birren, 1964).

It is understandable that an adult of 55 or older may become more inflexible, she/he may have had sufficient life experiences to decide how she/he will react or feel under most circumstances. Differences, then, do exist, and they need to be considered in designing programs for adults.

Winifred I. Warnat has formulated the following list of 10 characteristics of adult learners:

ADULT LEARNERS (Warnat, 1979)

1. *In terms of intelligence,* based on I.Q. we are smartest from eighteen to twenty-five years, but we are wiser and more experienced with increasing age.

2. At age forty-five, our vocabulary is three times greater than when we graduated from college.

3. At age sixty, our brain possesses almost four times as much information as when we were twenty-one.

4. *In terms of happiness and satisfaction with life,* we have the best physical sense of ourselves from ages fifteen to twenty-four.

5. We have the best professional sense of ourselves from ages forty to forty-nine.

6. Pessimism peaks between ages thirty and thirty-nine.

7. After age thirty, we become more realistic about achieving happiness; we realize that talent and determination

are not enough to guarantee success and that happiness is no longer a goal in itself, but encompasses our health, professional achievement, and emotional goals.

√8. *In terms of creativity,* generally the peak period is between the ages of thirty and thirty-nine, but varies according to profession.

√9. For the well-conditioned mind, there is no peak.

10. While the peak in most fields comes early, creative people continue to produce quality work throughout their lives.

These facts do not provide the adult educators with a precise map for designing programs. Yet two important conclusions do emerge:

1. Adult learners should be considered as adults (the learning program should be personalized); and

2. Knowing the age of a participant can be helpful in personalizing that learning program.

Research

Persons reviewing research studies on adults will find descriptions of what adults are like. For example:

Two lines of research specifically in the area of cognitive development have suggested that adults differ in their developmental status. First, there is increasing data which indicate that a large proportion of adults have not completed the transition between concrete (characterized by logical operations) and formal operational thought (characterized by propositional thinking) as evidenced on Piagetian tasks (Tomlinson-Keasy, 1972; Kuhn, Langer, Kohlberg, and Haan, 1971; Neimark, 1975) . . . .

Second, there is additional research that suggests a developmental sequence in thinking processes beyond Piaget's formal operations. The existence of a stage beyond formal operations was suggested on theoretical grounds by some authors (Riegel, 1973). More recently Kitchener (1977) has found evidence for the development of what she calls Reflective Judgment. This thinking process appears to build upon formal operations and go beyond it to allow individuals to make intelligent judgments in situations where information is incomplete.

In a group of 60 individuals, 20 high school juniors, 20 college juniors, and 20 advanced liberal arts graduate students, Kitchener found that there was a regular increase with *age* in scores on her measure of Reflective Judgment. In the graduate student population (an age group which approximates the age of many of those engaged in staff development) she found a range of Reflective Judgment scores from 2 to 7 on a 7-point scale. Thus, even in an adult population which one might assume would all have high scores on a measure of Reflective Judgment, wide variance was found.[10]

CMTI: Study One

To these studies we wish to add our recent research on a large group of adults who were in a structured learning experience. We (Andrews, Bryant, Houston) asked at the beginning of the study if it would be possible to find out how, why and under what circumstances adult learning occurs.

We have been fortunate in having the opportunity to complete two major studies of adult learning through a contract with Floyd Waterman, University of Nebraska, Omaha, for Teacher Corps. The first study was reported in *Designing Short-Term Instructional Programs*, available through the Association of Teacher Educators, Reston, Virginia. The second study is included in this volume.

Briefly stated, we studied the Corpsmember Training Institute (CMTI). CMTI was a three-week (eight hours a day) learning experience for 300 to 400 participants. The learners were divided into clusters with approximately 40 learners to a cluster and three faculty members assigned to each cluster. We designed and administered pretests and posttests on the cognitive objectives (the study of organizations, education that is multicultural, and community education). We also observed each cluster for three 20-minute periods each day.

On the basis of the analysis of the data in the first study, we learned that (Waterman):

- Achievement of a concept is not related to the amount of class time devoted to that concept; and

- Adults in process-oriented groups achieve more than those in task-oriented groups. Those in groups that are not clearly task- or process-oriented achieve least.

Both of these conclusions have implications for persons working with adults. The fact that achievement of a concept was not related to class time devoted to that concept is not consistent with what researchers have concluded about how young children learn. We wish to emphasize that all clusters studied the concepts; there was no control group which did not study the concepts.

The second conclusion is also of great interest. It means that instructors using more process approaches achieved greater adult cognitive gain. The process groups were characterized by group decisions. Instructional activities often included experiential activities. In the task clusters, achievement was stressed by instructors, objectives were clearly articulated with activities related to them, schedules were made and adhered to, and participants perceived that concepts were emphasized.

The implications of these two conclusions for teachers of adults are clear: repeated teaching of cognitive material will not lead to greater achievement, and when adults are more personally and actively involved in the learning situation, they learn more cognitive material.

CMTI: Study Two

In the study reported in detail in this volume, we examined these two conclusions (time-on-task and process vs. task) with a new population and a revised observation instrument. In order to deferentiate more narrowly between "task" and "process" clusters, we used an observation instrument which coded the three content areas into the following categories:

- Presentation — high cognitive
- Presentation — low cognitive
- Discussion — cognitive
- Experiential — cognitive

We also added two categories not related to content:

- Experiential — non-cognitive
- Non-instructional

Time-on-Task

In an analysis of the time-on-task data, we found there were several weak but consistent relationships between time, instruction, and achievement:

- Presenting low-cognitive material in multiculture and community was positively related to achievement of low-cognitive content in those areas.
- Presenting high-cognitive material in organization was positively related to high-cognitive achievement in organization.
- Presenting low-cognitive material in multiculture and community was positively related to total achievement in those areas.

Based on the data presented above, it was determined that *the relation was weak but positive between time devoted to instruction and adult achievement.* There appears to be a modest relation between time devoted to instruction of adults and their achievement, even when considering differences in content, levels of cognition, and methods of instruction.

Still, taken together, the two CMTI studies are far from conclusive as to the relation between time, instruction, and the achievement of adults.

The findings clearly question the raw importance of time as a major variable in adult achievement. The low relationships that were found account for less than 4 percent of the variance. Perhaps adults have developed individualized learning and coping styles that cloud any impact time would have on achievement. It could be hypothesized (and we so believe) that as people mature, they become more unalike, particularly with respect to the amount of time needed to learn cognitive concepts.

Process vs. Task

In investigating the presentation modes of the ten clusters we did find differences. However, we wish to emphasize that we did not find significant differences in achievement between or among the clusters. Therefore, any conclusions made should be very tentative.

In order to compare the time spent on the various presentation modes, we grouped together the five highest achieving clusters and the five lowest achieving. On three of the six categories they were almost equal:

- Presentation − low cognitive
- Discussion − cognitive
- Experiential − non-cognitive

On two of the categories, the highest achieving clusters spent more instructional time:

- Presentation − high cognitive
- Experiential − cognitive

In one category, the lowest achieving clusters spent more time:

- Non-instructional

These findings are consistent with our first study which reported that process clusters had greater achievement gains than did task clusters—the highest achieving clusters spent more time in experiential activities.

In this study, we created a distinction between high cognitive and low cognitive presentations. In the above comparisons, the highest achieving clusters spent more time in presenting high cognitive material.

In another section of our analysis we found that teaching experience was positively related to achievement of high cognitive concepts. Since the interns had little, if any, teaching experience, those with the teaching experience were the older adults, providing additional support for the stage theorists and possibly also for the "age" theorists. Considering the overall nature of the data from the two studies, one could conclude:

- Presentations of both low cognitive and high cognitive material are important for adults (research studies of young children often find correlations between low cognitive presentations and achievement; seldom, however, are correlations reported for high cognitive presentations).
- Experiential learning activities are helpful to adults in achieving cognitive gains.
- The amount of time spent teaching a cognitive fact has little relationship to whether or not the adult learns the concept.
- Non-instructional time has been correlated negatively to achievement in studies of children. Our study indicates that this may also be true for adults. In other words, adult teachers who spend too much time on non-instructional tasks (defined as periods of transition between activities, breaks for lunch of coffee/juice, administrative tasks, housekeeping activities and announcements) will have participants who have lower cognitive gains than adult teachers who spend less time on these activities.

Development Theory

Adult developmental theorists generally fall into two categories (Chickering, 1974; Bents, 1981):

1. *Adult Developmental Theorists*

   Believe that concerns, problems, and tasks are common to most or all adults at various times in their lives. With an understanding as to why these concerns loom more prominently at one time than another, Birren, Levinson, Gould, and Sheehy speak of adult development in terms such as life periods, passages, stages of life and periods of transition.

2. *Stage Developmental Theorists*

   Believe that there are distinct or qualitative differences in the structure (mode) of thinking at various times that are not age-related (Piaget, Kohlberg, Hunt, Sprinthall, Leevinger; Bents, 1981).

The theories are similar in some ways. The stage theorists believe one must go through stages of intellectual development in sequence; in other words, only older persons will have reached certain levels of development. Kohlberg, for example, has noted that "his data indicate that no adults have reached their two highest levels of moral development before ages 23 and 30, respectively."

We believe that both elements are important in understanding adults.

In order to more clearly describe our study of adults, we have developed the following "Phases of the Life Span," based in part upon that used by Birren (1964).

Duration of Phases of the Life Span

- Infant: Birth to two
- Preschool: Two to five
- Childhood: Five to twelve
- Adolescence: Twelve to seventeen
- Early Maturity: Seventeen to twenty-two
- Maturity: Twenty-two to forty
- Mid-Life: Forty to sixty
- Later Maturity: Sixty to death

The latter three phases, maturity, mid-life, and later maturity, are the focus of this study and analysis.

The major differences between youth and adult learners upon which we are basing our model have been described by Ann Fales and Mary Greey in "The Puzzle of Mid-Life Learning: What are the Pieces?" They maintain that people proceed to a mid-life point in a reasonably predictable pattern and because of life's influences, major changes occur during the mid-life phases. In developing the Phases of the Life Span above, we have been arbitrary about the specific ages. It is important to realize that the Mid-Life Phase could begin at an earlier or later age than that indicated on the chart.

Fales and Greey maintain that, "The first half of life . . . is enmeshed in taking care of business; establishing a secure base for independent existence; getting and keeping a means of livelihood; establishing a family, friends, and other support systems; gaining status and recognition in the community (Jung, 1971; Neugarten, 1968). People use the norms of important social groups, including parents, as valuable and needed sets of guidelines during these stages . . . a shift occurs from other-directed and conforming approaches to life toward greater autonomy and use of one's own psychological tasks of mid-life (Gould, 1978; Vaillant, 1977). There are many mid-life events which encourage this shift: aging or death of parents; the empty-nest; for women, often, a need to find their identity independent of traditional roles; for men an awareness of having attained, or failed to attain, one's dream (Levinson, 1978)."

Given this orientation, the authors have listed a set of characteristics of the pre-transitional adult:

1. A concern with approval from others (parents, peers, bosses, spouses, and even children);
2. An acceptance of one right way of doing things;
3. A preference for socially acceptable learning structures and methods;
4. Practical, concrete and goal-directed content interests.

These can be contrasted with the characteristics of the post-transitional adult:

1. A concern with self-approval—meeting one's own needs as perceived by oneself—a greater trust in one's intrinsic or "gut feeling" of what is right;
2. Consideration or acceptance of a variety of possible right answers;
3. A willingness to explore and use a wider range of learning approaches;
4. A greater interest in content areas other than those related to major social roles satisfactorily accomplished up to this point in life;
5. An increased interest in learning wholistically, whatever the subject matter.

Based upon these assumptions, certain principles for facilitating mid-life learning (really design principles) follow:

1. Pay attention to the individual learner;
2. Pay attention to the emotional, intuitive and sensation

modes of learning, as well as the thinking or cognitive
mode;
3. Teach self-awareness and reflective learning skills;
4. Value, in concrete ways, the experience of the individual learner;
5. Encourage acceptance of the idea that there are many
"right" ways to do things;
6. Give permission and support for the shift from other-
centered learning to self-centered learning;
7. Provide guidance regarding access to counselling and
psychotherapy where appropriate.

Design Principles

*Adults seldom learn, remember and use answers for
which they do not already have the question. . . .Effective
adult learning is an active search for meaning.*

We endorse this statement completely. As research has
shown, the older an adult is, the more inflexible he or she becomes. The adage about leading a horse to water may be an
appropriate analogy. If an adult does not want to learn, the
adult will not learn. This is equally true of children, but there
are major differences in motivation.

Children are motivated by the fun of learning (e.g., Sesame
Street), peer pressures, parent pressure, grades and most of all,
open or implied threats. "If you don't learn—whatever—you
will be a failure in the next grade, or not get into college, or
not get a job or be successful," etc. Such motivational approaches certainly apply to the young adult, but they seldom
apply to the adult who has passed the mid-transition period.
That person has become person-centered, his/her motivation
is intrinsic or non-existent. Therefore, it is particularly important for teachers of adults to understand what is motivating
those in their classes.

We realize that understanding motivation is difficult. An
adult may well share what she/he hopes to get out of an activity without revealing his/her real motivation. A major problem the designer of adult learning activities needs to consider

is whether or not the participants are required to attend. Certainly, the instructor should quickly find this out and make any adjustments that may be necessary. Since we believe that few if any adults learn anything if they are not personally interested, the instructor faces a much greater challenge in designing a program where all of the participants are required to attend. Also, finding out as much as possible about the participants can be helpful. Answers to questions such as age, number of children, marital status (married, divorced, widowed), occupation, etc., will assist the instructor of adults in understanding the participants.

On principle, then, we believe that certain special considerations should be given to designing adult programs.

In the previous sections we have looked at what is known about adults as learners, theories of adult development and research on adults. In closing, we wish to discuss three principles of design that are consistent with these data:

1. Data should be collected
2. Instruction should be personalized
3. Participants should be actively involved in their learning

In the following material, we are providing a brief description of a set of opening activities that can be used with any adult group which integrates these three principles.

Educators have talked about and tried to individualize instruction for children for many years. Researchers are now concluding that small group instruction is actually superior to individualization. We are neither refuting nor endorsing this concept. What we are suggesting for adults is personalization—a process of instruction in which the teacher sees each adult as a unique learner.

Adults are different (from each other, from the group, and from younger learners). The question for the teacher of adults is how to design an instructional program that recognizes the differences, while at the same time providing a learning experience for all participants. To do this, one must have data.

Data can be collected in a variety of ways and our suggestions are neither prescriptive nor all inclusive, but they may be helpful. In the following example, the instruction is personalized, data are collected, and the learners are actively involved.

Beginning an Adult
Learning Activity

I (5 minutes)

Before the first session begins, hand to each adult a 3x5 card and ask him/her to write on the card what each hopes to learn, experience or obtain as a result of participating in this activity. Encourage the participants to be truthful. Ask them *NOT* to put their names on the cards. Collect the cards.

II (5 minutes)

Explain the purpose of the activity. This should be a short presentation. The objectives, agenda, and requirements should be explained. These "givens" should also be put on newsprint, a chalk board, or on a handout.

III (10 minutes)

Then ask the participants working in groups of twos or threes to briefly share an experience relevant to the activity.

For example: Metric Education

Ask each person to write one reason why he/she is frustrated about metric education. Then in groups of twos or threes, have the participants discuss these.

Such requests can be positive or negative, but they must ask for a personal response.

During that time the instructor can read the cards collected at the beginning and quickly see if there are misunderstandings about the purpose of the activity.

IV (10 minutes)

Stop the group activity. Generally discuss the comments on the cards. Note those areas that will not be covered, explain why, and indicate the instructor's willingness to meet after the activity with anyone who wishes it for further discussion.

• • • •

These steps, taking only 30 minutes, at the beginning of any activity with adults are consistent with many of the findings previously reported.

1. The learner, by writing on the card, has to clarify his/her purpose for being there, and each response is totally personal.

2. The explication of the objectives, agenda, and requirements is helpful to those adults who desire structure and clarity.

3. The interaction groups provide everyone with an opportunity to speak, and to speak from personal experience. This is one way to provide experiential learning opportunities.

4. The instructor's review of the questions clarifies for him/her exactly what those in the activity expect (if necessary the activity can be redesigned). It also provides participants who have inappropriate expectations with an opportunity to leave before becoming either a problem to the instructor or personally frustrated.

The following three exhibits, compiled by Sara Massey, conceptualize in a helpful way much of what is known about adults as learners.

Exhibit One discusses the skills moderators need. Exhibit Two considers how to organize learning programs based on what the purpose of the instruction is. Exhibit Three illustrates the major components in the learning process.

The teachers of adults should find these three exhibits extremely valuable.

Conclusion

In this chapter we have brought together much of what is now known about adults as learners and have suggested some design features for teachers of adults. In our two studies we have made only a small contribution to the remaining, massive task of designing and reporting studies of adult learners. There are still far more questions unanswered than answered, but we do believe that enough is known now to improve the design of programs for adult learners. To that end, this report is dedicated.

REFERENCES

Bents, Richard H. and Howey, Kenneth R. "Staff Development —
  Change in the Individual," *Staff Development/Organization Development*, Alexandria, Va.: 1981 Yearbook Committee, Association
  for Supervision and Curriculum Development, 1981, pp. 12-16.

Birren, James E. *The Psychology of Aging.* Edgewood Cliffs, N.J.:
  Prentice-Hall, 1964, pp. 5-238.

Fales, Ann and Greey, Mary. "The Puzzle of Mid-Life Learning: What
  Are the Pieces?" *Yearbook of Adult and Continuing Education,
  1980-81 Sixth Edition*, Chicago, Illinois: Marquis Academic Media.
  (Reprinted from the Ontario Institute for Studies in Education,
  Toronto, Ontario.).

Knox, Alan B., ed. Enhancing Proficiency of Continuing Educators,
  New Directions for Continuing Education, No. 1. San Francisco:
  Jossey Bass Inc., 1979.

Massey, Sara R. "Staff Development: Teaching Adult Professionals,"
  Inservice, Syracuse, N.Y., National Council of States on Inservice
  Education, April, 1979.

Warnat, Winifred I., "A New Dimension of Adult Learning: Inservice
  Education," *Inservice*, Syracuse, N.Y., National Council of States on
  Inservice Education, April, 1979.

EXHIBIT ONE:

Skillful Moderators Know How To:

1. Initiate Discussions	Good discussions are sparked by key questions or statements that engage the person's imagination to relook, to see differently, or to connect new points.
2. Provide Information	Too many discussions occur in a vacuum without a focus point, a place to begin, and no input to keep them moving. The leaders seem to be saying, "I really don't know anything. What do you think?" A good moderator knows what information, how much, and when to give it to further the exploration of the participants.
3. Encourage Participation	Discussions are structured to insure ample opportunity to participate. Techniques to do this include: one-to-one rotating concentric circle, questions on cards collected and read by another person, oral completion of open statements around the room, small groups with specific open topics, etc.
4. Set Norms	There should be clear expectations for the discussion process: key points are written down, important information is shared, information is summarized, and all contributions are treated with respect.
5. Harmonize Differences	Differences of opinion and different perceptions are the essence of discussions, but the value of the discussion lies in finding the common goal, sorting the points of disagreement, focusing on the various answers, and keeping the group moving together toward the common goal.
6. Coordinate the Information	Links and connections must be made among speakers to keep the discussion focused and moving. The value of each person's contribution is in the relating of separate points to form the total.
7. Summarize the Decisions	If the time spent in discussion was of any value, there must be key points or something of importance which adds to the learning of participants. This needs to be clearly and concisely stated by someone.

EXHIBIT TWO:

The Learning Process

Awareness	Awareness sessions are usually introductions to a concept or technique. Participants rarely learn skills here but should leave the session with the information necessary for deciding whether they want to know more or whether the information presented could be useful in their work. Such sessions should be short—two hours at most—and exploratory in nature.
Skills	Participants should leave a skill session with at least one new skill. Trainer demonstration and participant practice with leadership shifting from the trainer to the participants is a common sequence. The length of the session depends on the complexity of the skill, but participants must leave knowing what they have learned.
Transfer of Skills	Learning a skill and trying it out on the job are two different activities. A "transfer" session best directly follows a skill-learning session. Providing both activities eliminates premature judgments like "my students won't do this," "this is dumb," or "I don't see how this will help in my work." Participants need to separate themselves as learners from themselves as workers and be given a safe situation to try out the skill. Then problems can be discussed on the basis of real experience.
Knowledge	Knowledge sessions include facts, theories, concepts, and ideas. The most successful knowledge sessions include exploration, participation in short experiments, structured observations, and reading interspersed with a number of structured reflections. The lecture that holds the attention well enough or long enough to achieve understanding is possible, but rare.
Attitude	Changing or developing attitudes is hard and at best can only occur through very intensive learning experiences over a five-day period or over a very long time period with less intense instruction.

EXHIBIT THREE:

The Content of Learning

1. Exploration	Participants need an opportunity to get acquainted with the content. Think of exploration as getting participants to view the goods before the auction starts rather than just waiting for them to be put up, one by one. Participants can look at materials, skim articles, generate questions, or share opinions with others. Participants need time to get involved with the content in their own way if useful learning is to occur.
2. Interaction	Participants' own experiences, feelings, and attitudes form the base for the most important learning experiences. Interaction is a way of removing participants from their relative isolation, getting input from other perspectives, and, furthering thinking. Variable grouping patterns—among friends, strangers, pairs, small group and large group—are necessary to encourage the most productive interaction.
3. Active Participation	Twenty minutes is as long as most of us can sit in one place without fidgeting. Even concerts have intermissions. The need of all participants for physical movement and use of senses is often forgotten in adult learning. Just changing groups provides some movement. Activities which demand active listening, rather than passive listening, will increase the alertness and, therefore, the learning of most groups.
4. Reflection and Articulation	Reflection must remain open ended with no expectation of "right" or "wrong" responses and serve as a vehicle for clarification and understanding. A do-stop-think process is necessary to make sense of activity that can otherwise be perceived as isolated and useless. Reflecting and articulating by participants on what, how, and why of the activity raise learning from the unconscious to a conscious level.
5. Synthesis or Integration	Time is most often the major factor in synthesizing, and it cannot be programmed to occur. For participants to integrate new learning with what they already know, a task or assignment to be done later is helpful. Comparing past with present also furthers this process. Without synthesis, each new technique, skill, or concept becomes just one more "innovation."

Chapter 2

THE TRAINING INSTITUTE

- *Theodore E. Andrews*

Introduction

CMTI is the commonly used acronym for Corpsmember Training Institute, a three-week workshop sponsored by Teacher Corps, United States Office of Education, and attended by Interns and Team Leaders beginning their two-year program.

Teacher Corps was created in 1965 to strengthen educational opportunities for children in areas with high concentrations of low income families, to encourage colleges and universities to broaden their programs of teacher preparation and to support demonstration programs of the training and restraining of experienced teachers and teacher aides.

During 1974-75, Teacher Corps, faced with a national shift in educational priorities from preservice to inservice, reduced the number of Interns (prospective teachers) in each of its projects to four (the previous average had been over 20). For the first time, Teacher Corps, with approximately 50 projects funded each year, for a two-year cycle, had the opportunity to bring together all of its Interns in one place for an extended learning experience to address problems highlighted in over ten studies completed on previous Teacher Corps cycles. These studies identified training voids that existed at the local projects. In particular, the studies revealed a need to emphasize the study of organizations and the richness of our nation's multicultural heritage and to provide a theoretical framework for the study of teaching and learning styles.

"*Additionally,*" stated William Smith, Director of Teacher Corps, "*project directors were reporting that Teacher Corps Interns needed an 'esprit de corps,' a personal identification with the national program effort. It also seemed to directors that a common training session could be the most realistic and profound cross-cultural learning and living experience ever provided by the Teacher Corps.*"

As a result of these feelings, and in order to meet its federal mandates, Teacher Corps conceived of the unique CMTI program. The first CMTI took place on the campus of University of Richmond, in Richmond, Virginia, in July 1975. The contract was awarded to the University of Nebraska at Omaha and Floyd Waterman was appointed as director.

The four-week Richmond program addressed two of the gaps noted in the evaluations of Teacher Corps—a two week emphasis on the study of organizations under the direction of Ron Corwin and Roy Edelfelt, and two weeks devoted to the study of teaching and learning styles under the direction of Bruce Joyce.

In April of 1976, a contract again was awarded to Floyd Waterman, University of Nebraska, Omaha, to serve as Director for the second CMTI, held at Florida State University. Jack Gant, of that University, agreed to serve as Instructional Leader with Roger Pankratz, Western Kentucky University, and JoAnne Taylor, Pepperdine University, serving as Curriculum Coordinators. The second CMTI was held in August 1976. The emphasis during the three week instructional program was again on the study of organizations, and teaching and learning styles. In addition, a multicultural strand was added.

The third national CMTI in Teacher Corps' twelve years of operation featured representatives from 56 projects and took place on July 10 through 30, 1977 at San Diego State University in San Diego, California. Again, the contractor was The University of Nebraska at Omaha with Floyd Waterman as Director. Roger Pankratz served as the Instructional Leader.

Following a one-year gap (when no new interns entered Teacher Corps) the next CMTI was planned.

The fourth CMTI (described in this publication) was also held at San Diego State University from June 17 to July 7, 1979. Floyd Waterman served as both the Project Director and Instructional Leader.

1979 CORPSMEMBER TRAINING INSTITUTE

In 1979, all Program 78 Team Leaders arrived in San Diego, California on June 9. Interns arrived one week later, on June 16. During their week alone, the Team Leaders were given training in the Santa Barbara supervisory training materials. After the Interns arrived, the three-week CMTI offered a common curriculum to both groups. That curriculum concentrated on concepts in the areas of organizational theory, education that is multicultural, and community-based education. One hour each day was also spent on an "Instructional Analysis Component," to provide an opportunity for Interns and Team Leaders to reflect on the instructional strategies used used at the Institute.

William L. Smith, Director, Teacher Corps, described the nature of CMTI:

CMTI is a culturally pluralistic living and learning community. The institute must have substance and a theoretical foundation. From that foundation, the institute must deal with low-income schools and their students. It will also be important to incorporate the community into the institute; it must be seen from an organizational perspective, and it must be seen as a learning resource.

When the CMTI participants leave the institute, they will go to projects, where they will spend the bulk of their time in schools, with children. Additionally, they will have university coursework and community activities for which they are responsible. They will be extremely busy. Thus, CMTI should be an academically rigorous experience. Equally important, since they will be very busy with day-to-day tasks in the porject, participants of CMTI should be allowed to develop conceptual frameworks and to reflect on new concepts.

CMTI was "a culturally pluralistic living and learning environment." It can be viewed as a community made up of the many diverse ethnic and cultural populations which the Teacher Corps serves. At the same time, CMTI provided an environment in which to learn certain basic concepts in the areas of organizational theory, education that is multicultural, and community-based education. Further, the learning and living aspects of the CMTI were structured to reflect and reinforce one another.

CMTI, like the Teacher Corps, concentrated on the study of content which would prepare Corpsmembers to work in schools and communities in appropriate roles, as learners. The CMTI, as an initial Teacher Corps experience, attempted to get Corpsmembers ready to enter and learn in their local project settings.

CMTI also offered the opportunity for reflection and academic rigor in a child-free environment. CMTI offered few of the distractions which Corpsmembers would encounter in their local projects. Thus, there was time to build a Corpsmember team, a cohesive group which would have some sense of its common purpose. Additionally, CMTI offered time for reflection on new learning and experience.

General CMTI Outcomes

CMTI's content and design were based on the following premise:

CMTI participants, over the next two years, will function as learners and actors within a very complex system. That system is made up of subsystems and a variety of organizations. Those include such diverse organizations as a local education agency, an institution of higher education, a community, a state education agency, and Teacher Corps-Washington, all operating within the context of our larger social milieu. Each of those organizations in turn is made up of subsystems. All of those systems and organizations interact and impact on each other.

Further, the institute designers made three assumptions:

1. Interns and Team Leaders can be most effective if they enter and function in their local projects, with their many complex systems, as a team of *learners*.

2. There is a set of identifiable concepts in the CMTI subject areas (i.e. organizational theory, community-based education, and educational that is multicultural) which has proven useful in learning about and understanding such complex systems.

3. There is a set of skills embedded in the CMTI subject areas which, when mastered, will be useful to Interns and Team Leaders as they enter and participate in such complex systems.

Next, the institute designers posited the following two beliefs:

1. Understanding and functioning appropriately in the complex socio-structural context alluded to above is prerequisite to individuals' study, mastery, and application of effective teaching and learning processes in schools.

2. One highly effective strategy for introducing basic teaching and learning processes is the modeling of effective instruction. Further, discussion or debriefing of modeled practices is extremely helpful as an introduction to pedagogical effectiveness.

Finally, the institute designers sought to address some less tangible and less clearly academically-oriented concerns which are nonetheless intrinsic to the Teacher Corps and to the pluralistic populations which the program seeks to serve.

These relate primarily to Teacher Corps processes, concerns, and purposes.

The intended outcomes of CMTI were described as follows:

Teacher Corps Processes and Concerns

- CMTI participants will understand the Teacher Corps as a national program.
- CMTI participants will develop an esprit de corps which reflects the nation-wide presence of the Teacher Corps.
- CMTI participants will be prepared to join in the local project's team-building processes.

The CMTI Experience

- CMTI participants will experience a multicultural living environment.
- CMTI participants will experience, observe, and analyze a wide variety of teaching and learning approaches.

Content Areas

- CMTI participants will know and understand basic concepts related to organizational theory, community-based education, and education that is multicultural.
- CMTI participants will develop the skills necessary to apply those concepts in schools, communities, and universities.
- CMTI participants will develop appropriate project entry skills and attitudes.

The CMTI Instructional Philosophy

The institute designers also identified several philosophical stances which guided CMTI development as follows:

- The primary obligation to the CMTI community is to learn and to help others learn.
- Instructional sequencing of process developmental skills, involving all the domains of learning, yields a more positive and productive learning climate.

• The opportunity for growth is greatly enhanced by promoting norms of:

  — risk-taking,
  — experimentation,
  — dealing with conflict openly, and
  — succeeding and failing.

 • There are skills and knowledge which can be learned and applied that are critical to individual group learning at all levels. Some of them are:

  — listening skills as a prerequisite to recognizing the uniqueness of others;
  — giving and receiving feedback;
  — the ability to describe behavior without interpreting it;
  — problem identification skills (avoiding reliance on solution orientation); and
  — observation skills as a means of sharpening the ability to learn from others.

  • Cognitive learning and affective growth are complementary.

 • When appropriate human interaction experiences are planned, the learning potential for the total group is greater than the individual contributions.

  • Readiness for learning is, in part, dependent upon the creation of a helping relationship.

Population of Study

The Institute was organized into ten clusters. Each cluster was composed of about 40 participants and three instructors. The participants in a cluster included all interns and their team leaders from eight projects. Projects included in each cluster were assigned in advance to create cultural diversity and geographical spread. Characteristics of individuals were not known nor considered in making these assignments;

thus, no systematic bias toward specific characteristics of participants that might have influenced results was generated.

Each of the ten clusters had specific space assigned to it on the campus of San Diego State University. Six of the clusters had rooms in the Aztec Center, a student commons building. These rooms tended to be open, carpeted, large, and ideal for a variety of instructional activities. The other four clusters met in nearby buildings in traditional classrooms. These rooms tended to be cramped and uncarpeted. In addition to the assigned space, all clusters were free to use the outside campus areas if they wished. The almost perfect San Diego weather made this option possible.

The clusters met daily from 8:00 a.m. until 5:00 p.m. with an hour free for lunch. Individual clusters were able to use the time as they wished with the exception of the Instructional Analysis hour set aside at the end of each day.

In addition to the cluster staff, five content specialists were present throughout the three weeks. They made presentations to individual clusters on an individual basis and assisted the cluster staffs in developing content-specific instructional material.

Demographic information on participants is summarized in Table 1. This includes data on role, age, sex, marital status, and race/ethnicity. Twenty (20) percent of participants were team leaders while 77 percent were interns. Interns generally had never taught while team leaders were selected for their teaching experience and ability. The concepts of the institute, however, were equally new to both.

The model age for participants was 20-24 years while 63 percent were 29 or younger. Team leaders tended to be older, as a group, than interns. Over two-thirds of the participants were female and 60 percent were single.

Forty-two (42) percent of the participants were white and 34 percent were black. Thirteen percent were Hispanic Americans, 7 percent Native Americans and 7 percent Asian Americans.

The research study which follows is based on this population.

Table 1: Population of the Study

Variable	Frequency	Percent
Role		
Team Leader	79	20
Intern	299	77
Other	8	2
Age		
20-24 years	150	39
25-29 years	93	24
30-34 years	61	16
35-39 years	40	10
40 - over	42	11
Sex		
Female	275	69
Male	125	31
Marital Status		
Married	154	40
Single	232	60
Race/Ethnicity		
White	163	42
Black	130	34
Asian	14	4
Native American	28	7
Hispanic American	51	13

Chapter 3

A REVIEW OF THE LITERATURE
IN SELECTED AREAS
OF EDUCATIONAL RESEARCH

● *Brenda L. Bryant*

What improves student learning? The answers to this question trigger innovations for the classroom. The question itself has stimulated much in the way of educational research in recent years. While new knowledge continues to be contributed to the literature, in fact, little is known about the effectiveness of teaching. Slowly, discoveries are being made. This chapter describes some of those discoveries about teaching and learning with specific emphasis given to research on teacher effectiveness, instructional methods, time-on-task and student attending behavior, student characteristics affecting learning, and the adult learner.

Teacher Effectiveness

A number of educational researchers have attempted to identify teacher effects or teacher behaviors which contribute to student achievement. The intention of this search is to isolate and describe the variables of teaching that lead to improved student performance.

In a paper prepared for the American Association of Colleges for Teacher Education, Donald Medley (1977) reports on 289 studies of teacher effectiveness which is defined, customarily, as teacher behaviors related to student achievement. Examining the literature on elementary school teachers working with students of low socio-economic status, Medley states that the effective third grade teacher devotes more time to task-related or academic activities than does the ineffective teacher. The effective teacher spends more time with large groups, provides individual attention, and asks more lower order questions than the ineffective teacher. Independent work without the teacher present yields lower achievement gains and higher achievement is produced in classrooms where pupils are observed to engage in less deviant or disruptive behavior.

Some differences are evident when teachers work with students of higher socio-economic status. Effective teachers of these students provide less individual attention to pupils and are more likely to discuss pupils' answers to questions.

Although there are fewer data available for students above grade three, Medley concludes from the literature that the effective teacher in the upper elementary grades talks more, keeps pupils on task, is less permissive, asks easy, low-order questions, is more selective in the use of criticism, allows more pupil automony, and favors less traditional materials than his/her counterparts whose students fail to achieve as well. These findings describe the traditional teacher, although it must be remembered that the implications are not well supported.

In four separate investigations (Rouk, 1979) Robert and Ruth Soar have observed 154 elementary school classrooms for trends that indicate how learning is influenced by classroom emotional climate and teacher management of instruction. Their findings acknowledge, not surprisingly, that a negative climate characterized by severe criticism and rebuking is not conducive to learning. On the other hand, the Soars did not produce data to suggest that a positive, warm classroom climate does much to increase student achievement.

The greatest achievement gains appear to take place in classrooms falling in the middle range—"where emotional climate is essentially neutral." (p.8) Additionally, the Soars report that the greatest student achievement gains occur in classrooms where the teacher uses only a moderate amount of any one "good" behavior and creates a balance between student self-direction and teacher control of learning activities. It appears that some degree of structure and limit setting is functional; teachers who tightly structure student learning and focus on task produce achievement gains in low-level tasks such as memorization, while students who are permitted more freedom and choice gain more in the way of complex and abstract learning.

Frederick McDonald (1975), reporting the Phase II results of the Beginning Teacher Evaluation Study (BTES), finds little evidence that one teaching method is better than another; instead, a pattern of techniques characterizes the effective teacher and those techniques vary from grade to grade and subject to subject. Effective second grade teachers of reading interact with individual pupils, work with groups and use a variety of materials while the factors related to achievement in second grade mathematics are the amount of instructional content and the amount of time spent on the content. In teaching reading to fifth graders the most effective instructional activity is continuous reading of complex materials and in teaching mathematics to fifth graders it is the range of content covered, the use of group instruction, and longer periods of student-teacher interaction that affects student achievement. In examining the BTES results, E. Joseph Schneider (1980) stresses the importance of dual goals of teaching: keeping the student on task and performing tasks at a high success rate.

As a result of the Texas Teacher Effectiveness Project, Brophy and Evertson (1975) write that the effective elementary school teacher is a good classroom manager and that learning proceeds smoothly without excessive cognitive strain. The teacher has confidence in the ability of the students to learn, is willing to change the curriculum as needed, engages in diagnostic activities, carefully demonstrates new material and spends time observing and working with individual students. Brophy and Evertson were surprised to discover that lower-order, short questions are used by effective teachers and that discussion correlates negatively with learning which suggests that the lecture method may be effective.

Based on an examination of the process of teaching basic reading skills in secondary schools, Jane Stallings (1979) advises teachers "to get the show on the road when the bell rings and stay supportive." Effective teachers discuss homework on the reading content; they provide instruction in new work; they provide drill and practice and encourage oral reading. While instruction is focused on the small or total group, the teacher uses praise, support, positive corrective feedback, and short quizzes. On the other hand, ineffective teachers perform more management tasks, permit outside intrusions, social interactions, misbehavior or negative interactions. They offer students choices, expend too much time on writing assignments and silent reading and they work too frequently with one student at a time. Stallings also reports that class size is related to student achievement given different ability groups.

Barak Rosenshine (1975b) arrives at similar conclusions in reviewing the literature on achievement of elementary students from low socio-economic backgrounds. Positive significant results are achieved when instruction is direct, factual questions are asked, the teacher provides positive feedback, study in groups is supervised, and students attend to the task.

After examining four communications models used successfully to promote positive self concept, William Overman (1979) concludes that the teacher who confronts students is nonjudgmental, uses participatory problem solving, and obtains commitments from students is likely to reduce discipline problems and increase learning in the classroom. Keith Main (1979) lists mutual respect, shared responsibility, skill as a facilitator, learner involvement in objective setting, moderate structure, mutual inquiry, small groups, and a flexible environment as the factors leading to fulfillment for adult learners.

In a longitudinal study of the teaching effectiveness of teacher education graduates at Western Kentucky University, Sandefur and Adams (1975) report that good teaching is characterized by maximum student involvement in experiential situations, maximum student freedom, and personal traits described as warmth, democratic attitude, affective awareness and a personal concern for students. Fitzmaurice (1976) confirms that teacher attitudes directly influence student progress; Blair (1975) asserts that teacher effort in reading instruction is associated with student achievement in reading in the primary and middle grades; Wilson and Koran (1975) stress the importance of active behavior on the part of students learning science.

Ramirez (1978) examines the effectiveness of teachers teaching reading in Spanish and concludes that positive effects are emphasizing decoding skills, explaining grammatical rules, encouraging oral reading of short segments and correcting pupil errors. Factors affecting achievement negatively are teacher questions concerning details, explanations of vocabulary out of context and the practice of students reading entire paragraphs orally. In Follow Through classes, Jane Stallings (1976) reports that a teacher's use of higher cognitive questions may not lead to improved performance for all students. Rather, the context of the situation in which questions are asked may be more important than skill in asking higher order questions. When teachers develop a variety of materials and provide differentiated instruction, Blair (1976) discovers a rise in student achievement. The role of the teacher is of interest to Amster (1975) who states that junior high school students taught by peer teachers or regular teachers achieve more than students taught by specialists or exchange teachers. For optimum teaching efficiency, the teaching rate in higher education should be an average between fast and slow according to Kuhlman-Wilsdorf (1975).

A number of teacher behaviors may appear to affect achievement. Some studies, however, are inconclusive; others are contradictory. One factor affecting achievement currently is receiving much attention. That factor is time spent engaged in learning.

Time on Task and Attending Behavior

Quoting Benjamin Bloom, "Time is the central variable in school learning," a recent edition of the American School Board Journal (Fowler, 1977) asks what school board members and school administrators can do either to increase the amount of time schools offer for instruction or to ensure that the time available is spent effectively teaching children (p. 26). The question reflects knowledge of several current studies which point to time and student attending behavior as essential factors in learning. Attending, according to Gagné (1976), is a process which "serves the function of modifying the information flow from the sensory register to the short-term memory. The array of stimulation that reaches the learner through his sensory register is acted upon selectively by means of this process, in such a way that certain salient features of it are 'attended to' and 'perceived' " (p. 26).

Convincing arguments are made concerning time attending to task as evidenced in this remark by Borg (1979) . . . "schooling does make a difference. When research over the past thirty-six years shows consistent positive relationships between time on task and achievement, and when we find sixteen studies differing in virtually every aspect of design and yet yielding consistent positive results, we can, in fact, be very confident that the relationships found are real and enduring" (p. 7). Three of these studies are discussed by Barak Rosenshine (1976) who states that the stronger the academic emphasis, the stronger the academic results. He cites Robert Soar who finds that time spent on reading and numbers is associated with growth in those areas and that no non-academic activity yields positive correlations with reading and mathematics achievement. Discussing the work of Brophy and Evertson, Rosenshine says that in low socio-economic classrooms time spent on seatwork or individualized activities is positively related to achievement and time spent on oral responding is negatively related. The opposite result is obtained in high socio-economic status classrooms. Evidently academic time is important, but the content of that time is an important factor as well. Stallings and Kaskowitz, as reviewed by Rosenshine, produce clear results. The time teachers spend on interactions regarding reading or mathematics materials is consistently and usually significantly related to achievement.

For Donald Medley (1977) the effective third grade teacher of low socio-economic status classroom devotes more time to task-related or academic activities and the effective upper grade teacher keeps pupils on task. Pupil attention to the subject of the lesson is positively correlated to achievement for both low and high socio-economic students. In a 1975 publication Frederick McDonald reports that second grade reading achievement is related to time spent. The Beginning Teacher Evaluation Study has introduced the notion of Academic Learning Time (ALT) which is defined as the amount of time a student spends attending to academic tasks while also performing at a high success rate. "The more ALT a student accumulates, the more he/she can be assumed to be learning" (BTES, 1978), (p. 1). In an updated paper, Rosenshine and Berliner introduce the term academic engaged time. Their primary finding is that "student time spent engaged in relevant content appears to be an essential variable for which there is no substitute" (p. 12). Benjamin Bloom cites fifteen studies in which student attention is correlated with academic gain. Ward and Tikunoff (1975) reveal that extra individual or tutoring time is helpful in improving student performance. Frederick, Walberg, and Rasher (1979) report that high schools with higher reading achievement have a lower amount of lost time and more positive comments are used by the teacher.

Two studies raise questions about the importance of engaged time on task. Relying on the logs maintained by fifth grade teachers, Smith (1979) questions if time allocated for social studies instruction accounts for variance in student achievement. The result is a very slight relationship between allocated time and achievement. "The usefulness of allocated time as a potent variable in planning or evaluation of instruction seems questionable" (p. 36). Borg (1979) cites Good and

Beckerman (1978) who find relatively small differences in on-task behavior between high and low achievers. Involvement is higher in tasks assigned by the teacher and in large or small group activities where the teacher is present. The variation in on-task behavior from classroom to classroom suggests the importance of the relationships between teacher behavior and pupil work involvement (p. 6).

Teacher Moves and Methods

Closely related to the examinations of teacher effects (specific behaviors) are studies of the effectiveness of various teaching methods (sets of behaviors). "Teaching methods are recurrent instructional processes, applicable to various subject matters, and usable by more than one teacher" (Berliner and Gage, 1976, p. 5). While research on teacher effects has been largely limited to elementary school, research on instructional methods has been conducted with the primary grades through adult education. The findings are summarized below.

Much of the research on teaching methods is inconclusive. In analyzing research studies conducted between 1908 and 1974, Weimer (1974) concludes that there is no clear evidence of a single superior method of teaching. Comparing verbal teaching methods to non-verbal methods in grade four mathematics, Hollingsworth (1973) finds no significant differences between treatments. The lecture and discussion methods are of interest to Johnson (1976) who reviews the relevant research and finds no significant differences between the two methods. No significant difference is the result of a study by Newman (1974) who compared the effectiveness of programmed instruction, tutored/programmed instruction and the lecture/demonstration methods in teaching basic Algebra. Murphy (1977) writes that "there have been several hundred studies comparing one teaching method to another, and the overwhelming portion of these studies show few if any differences" (p. 9). Undergraduate students taking a course in special education do about equally well with modularized, self-paced instruction, or modularized, self-paced instruction with supplementary lectures and discussions, or with the traditional method, although McCarney and Bullock (1977) believe that the former two approaches might prove more effective. The ability of graduate students to interpret research, states Maxim (1977), is improved with both the structured instructional approach or the inquiry-based instructional approach.

In spite of the lack of any preferred instructional method, several researchers cautiously endorse a more structured approach to teaching. Looking at teachers of first and third graders, Stallings (1975) reports that the highly controlled classroom environment in which teachers use systematic instruction and positive reinforcement contributes to higher scores in reading and mathematics. Flexible classroom environments that provide more exploratory materials and allow for more choice contribute to higher scores on the test of non-verbal reasoning, to lower absence rates, and to a willingness on the part of children to work independently. Although he points to some difficulty in recommending it, Rosenshine (1975c) supports direct instruction where the teacher is the dominant leader who decides on activities and conducts instruction without giving reasons. At the community college level Reimanis (1972) finds that the superior teaching approach is a structured class which provides student-centered learning contrasted against instructor-directed, unstructured classes. In the precollege psychology classroom, Stahl (1976) describes four categories of technical teaching skills that are seen to be effective in instructional behavior. They are, first, organizational class moves where the focus of the lesson is outlined or reviewed; second, structuring class moves where the teacher establishes a context for information; third, conditional class moves where premises are linked to consequent statements; and fourth, wait-time class moves where the teacher uses silence. All four moves suggest a directed approach to teaching.

Even with evidence to support directed or structured classrooms, methodology remains in question. The study reported in this document is concerned with three general instructional methods: lecture, discussion, and experiential learning. Each is examined below from the perspectives of the available research.

- Lecture Method (Direct presentation)

Probably the lecture method is more effective in transmitting cognitive information. Olander and Robertson (1973) report that fourth grade mathematics pupils taught by the expository approach are significantly better in computation and pupils taught by the discovery approach are better in retaining the ability to apply mathematics and have a more positive attitude toward the subject. At the college level Bligh (1971) examines direct presentation methods including live lecture, recorded lecture and written lecture and concludes that with reservations it seems possible that the use of the recorded lectures results in deeper thinking than the use of live lectures or the reading of prescribed texts. However, there is no difference in achievement at the simpler cognitive levels when any of the three methods is used. Bravlio (1971) distinguishes between vertical or didactic approaches and horizontal or experiential approaches and concludes that among adults success with the two orientations is culturally based. Hispanic students are more likely to succeed with the vertical approach; Anglos are more likely to succeed when the horizontal approach is used. In his examination of the direct presentation for adults Kreitlow (1976) finds the lecture gives the most consistent results in learner outcomes and that the presence of the live researcher enhances the effectiveness of the lecture. The use of film is close to the live lecture on results. Leifer (1976) concludes that television and film can be used to teach cognitive, social, and emotional content and information-processing skills to students ranging in age from preschool to adult provided that the media is carefully planned into the learning program. Lecturing to twelfth grade mathematics students produces greater achievement than the use of games (Warren, 1973). The objectives of health instruction are found to be achieved equally well using values clarification or lecture techniques (Weber, 1978). In the teaching of family relationships to college students, the concept method produces greater acquisition, transfer, and retention of knowledge than the expository method (Hoover, 1974).

In short, the lecture is efficient and effective in transmitting knowledge, but it may not be the most effective method to develop affective learning or build positive attitudes toward subject matter. McLeish (1976) finds that retention from lectures drops from 80 percent in eight weeks and that students can do as well on written tests without attending the course lectures, yet he states (p. 297):

> The lecture has its own specific virtues as a teaching method. These must be duly emphasized. By means of this technique the scholar can readily inspire an audience with his own enthusiasm; he can capture the imagination of his auditors by relating his special field to human destiny and human purposes; he can communicate research results and relate these to the practical and theoretical problems that bear on man's estate. The lecture method enables him to achieve these ends with the utmost economy of means. This accounts for its survival over two thousand years of higher education.

> Defined thus, however, the art of lecturing is a difficult one. To achieve the required standard of performance it seems obvious that both training and practice are essential. The lecturer needs to have at his disposal a variety of skills that do not come together as a result of natural endowment, except perhaps in exceptional cases.

- Discussion Method (Interactive)

The discussion method occurs when a group of persons assembles at a designated time and place to communicate interactively using speaking, non-verbal, and listening processes in order to achieve instructional objectives (Gall and Gall, 1976). In social studies classes in grades three, four, and five Armento (1977) finds that the more students verbally manipulate relevant concept dimensions, the stronger the achievement will be. Gage (et al, 1975) reports that the important variables in the recitation strategy in grade six are a high level of structuring, soliciting student recall, and reacting to students with praise and with reasons for incorrect answers when such responses occur. Twelfth graders achieve higher post-test scores when they are receiving individualized instruction. The lecture-discussion method is second in effectiveness followed by non-instruction (Oen and Sweany, 1971). In his review of the literature on college teaching, McKeachie (1971) asserts that discussions are more effective than lectures and that student-centered discussions are more effective than instructor-centered discussions for goals of retention, application, problem-solving, attitude change, and motivation. Dubin and Taveggia (1968) review thirty-six studies of the achievement of college students in both discussion and lecture courses. In the comparisons 51 percent favored the lecture method and 49 percent favored the discussion method. Although the methods are about equally effective, Dubin and Taveggia conclude that the discussion develops concepts and problem solving skills while the lecture is more efficient in the transmission of information. According to Gall and Gall (1976) the discussion method may be more effective than the more passive learning environment of the lecture if the teacher wants students to reflect on and confront their attitudes. In summary, they write (p. 213):

Why should teachers use the discussion method? They should use it because it is effective in promoting important educational objectives: mastery of subject matter content, especially mastery related to students' use of higher cognitive processes; attitude change, including development of positive attitudes

towards concepts taught in the curriculum; solving
of complex problems which require group commitment for implementation; and development of discussion skills related to listening, speaking, and
group leadership. Furthermore, these positive effects
have been observed in a variety of subject matter
areas. Although some educators think that the discussion method is more appropriate for teaching the
humanities and social sciences than for teaching
mathematics and the physical sciences, we find no
evidence to support this notion. The nature of the
intended learning outcome (for example, attitude
change), rather than the curriculum content, deter-
mines the effectiveness of the discussion method.

- Experiential Method (Active participation)

An experiential approach to teaching makes full and
extensive use of verbal and kinesthetic involvement of
the learner in activities such as simulations, games,
role plays, and psycho-dramas. Experiential activities
are likely to be more student-centered and self-directed
and to occur in individualized settings or in varying
group sizes more often than the lecture or discussion
methods. Since experiential methods are not likely to
be used to the exclusion of other methods, little comparative data exist. Seidner (1976) reviews the literature
on simulations and games and asserts that non-simula-
tion games are particularly appropriate for teaching
facts and concepts and that affective objectives can be
achieved through interactive simulations and role plays
where role empathy might be expected. Citing DeVries
and Edwards, Seidner (1976) reports findings suggesting that experiential techniques may improve relations
among children from varying social and ethnic backgrounds. Students, too, enjoy games and simulations
and, therefore, this method should be considered
highly motivating. Nevertheless, studies of cognitive
gain indicate that these techniques are no more effective than other techniques in producing knowledge

acquisition. Once knowledge is acquired, however, there is evidence to support the contention that better retention results from action-oriented environments. Olmstead (1970) reports that small group methods in general can be effective for enhancing motivation for learning, developing positive attitudes toward the later use of course materials, and improving problem-solving skills. Although no more effective than the lecture for transmitting information and concepts, small group methods help increase the student's depth of understanding.

Several methods are appropriate teaching tools. Robert Segal (1947) supports selection of the best method for instructional purpose and emphasizes the student-teacher relationship as the key factor influencing success for the learner. "Teaching is less an intellectual than a social affair." (p. 21). The emotional climate of the classroom is critical to the effectiveness of the method—whatever method is used.

Student Characteristics

The above data suggest that no one method is more effective than another and any method may be most effective given the right circumstances. What are the circumstances which contribute to a method's effectiveness? Much of the literature points to student characteristics as the important variable. In other words, a method's effectiveness depends upon the characteristics of the learner. Ward and Tikunoff (1975) write, "Effective teaching probably centers around when a skill is used, with whom, for what purpose, within what form of total instructional situation rather than presence or absence of the skill." (p. 22) Berliner and Rosenshine (1975) believe that "at the level of the individual student, teaching methods have different potential for affecting knowledge acquisition."

In a study of first grade reading by Donovan and Austin (1978) results indicate that pupils whose modality preferences are congruent with the primary instructional focus of initial reading programs achieve significantly higher scores on all measures of initial reading behavior than do pupils whose modality preferences are not congruent with the instructional focus. Elliott (1975) in an exploratory study supports the notion of adult learning styles observing that participants have their own particular ways of moving through lessons.

Several studies report different student responses based on the students' socio-economic status (Medley, 1977; Brophy and Evertson, 1975; Soar and Soar, 1974; Roenshine, 1975b). Bravlio (1971) says cultural background is an important factor. Berliner (1976) notes that student performance in different curriculum areas is differentially affected by student background characteristics and that when students bring learnings from home to school the school program has less impact than it does when the subject is taught totally in school. McDonald (1976) confirms the variations among effective teaching techniques when he compares second and fifth grade student performance in reading and mathematics. At the college level McKeachie (1971) finds that different methods appear to work well with different students. Again at the undergraduate level McCarney and Bullock (1977), believe that "What is needed is research that would demonstrate the appropriate instructional method for each student. . . . When this type data can be gathered, student achievement should then be maximized." (p. 328). Finally, Brophy (1975) encourages researchers "to shift attention from searches for effective teachers or even effective teaching to searches for reliable cause and effect relationships" (p. 15).

The conclusions are evident. For the above researchers, teacher effects and teaching methods must be tied to student characteristics if more important differences in teaching and learning are to be found. It appears that socio-economic status, cultural background, the subject matter or curriculum being taught, and the students' learning styles may all affect achievement. Age, too, may be a factor— one to be discussed independently.

Adult Learning

The study reported in this document investigates student achievement, time engaged on task, and teaching methods employed by the instructional teams. Unlike the subjects of many previous studies where these variables are considered, the population of this study is comprised of adults ranging in age from 20 to 40+. In the preceding section it became evident that student characteristics have an important effect on learning. Therefore, it is necessary to understand the adult learner and the unique impact of increasing age on academic performance.

"Adults as learners are different from children as learners in self-concept, in their experience, in orientation to learning, and in readiness to learn," says Malcolm Knowles (Thompson, 1970, p. 56). In his review of the literature, Widman (1975) asserts that adults exhibit more ease at the task of concept formation than do youngsters. As age increases so does movement from concrete to abstract and the ability to differentiate among concepts. Adults use visual processes to learn and create potent images for themselves. They conceptualize functionally rather than physically which leads to a focus on purpose as opposed to appearance.

Educators, theorists, and researchers characterize the adult learner with similar descriptors. They are self-directed (Knowles, 1970), (Thompson, 1970), self-rewards (McLagan, 1975), and feedback (Beyer, 1975), (Fincher, 1976). Looking for immediate application of their learning, adults elect relevant, job-related educational experiences (Knowles, 1973) that avoid time wasting abstractions and encourage economizing on time (Forman, 1976). "There is a tendency during adulthood for a greater task orientation and for a set or expectancy that emphasizes accuracy in learning tasks" (Knox, 1977), (p. 434). The importance of task and accuracy is reinforced by Beyer (1975) who finds undergraduates learn more and are more enthusiastic when engaged in mastery learning and by Dauzat (1978) who observes the greatest achievement gains for adults in basic education programs when they are involved in competency-based instruction.

Adults, however, should not be viewed as a like set of learners. Perhaps even more so than among individual children, differences among adults are vast. McLagan (1975) cautions the designers of adult education programs to be aware of individual differences. Self-esteem, meaningfulness of various goals, clarity of self-image, and perceived locus of control differ from person to person and can greatly affect learning. The differences can mean that some learners respond best to structure while others prefer freedom to learn on their own. Similarly Even (1973) tells the adult educator to provide activities aimed at individual and group effectiveness and Boracks (1978) stresses the need to provide adult learners with procedures *and* to promote the use of their own procedures as well.

Adult Basic Education students are observed by Manzo (1975) to appear highly aggressive and cautious about intimacy with others and to display a slight degree of social-emotional dependency. They exhibit a sense of fragileness and a need for a healthy release from tensions. Long, McCrary, and Ackerman (1979) caution that what is learned in childhood may not be maintained through adulthood. Therefore, they support the application of Piagetian theory to adult learning.

In surveying rural adults McCannon finds this student population to be primarily females who pursue personal development and who are not seeking academic credit. Urban adults tend to be males in vocational learning for academic credit.

As a whole adult learners seem to differ from children and present some common preferences for learning strategies among themselves. As individuals they are unique and in need of instruction that recognizes differences in experience, self-concept, goals and learning styles. It should be no surprise that teaching methods recommended for adults accommodate to independence and variation. In a training course utilizing self-direction, experiential learning, and a problem-centered curriculum, workers improve their self-actualizing tendencies and prefer participatory training experiences (Gilford, 1975). In a literature review Collican (1974) reports increasing evidence that adults plan a great deal of learning for themselves without any assistance or intervention from professional adult educators. Furthermore, group learning is perceived as not fulfilling personal goals. Therefore, Collican supports packaged programs for independent learning. Malcolm Knowles (Thompson, 1970) recommends constructing a process design for adults as opposed to a content design. Involvement of participants in program planning, an adult social atmosphere, diagnosis of learning needs, sequential learning experiences, a plan of specific activities, and evaluation are the components of a process design (p. 56). Based on a review of the literature, Schiavone (1978) selects an individualized, diagnostic-prescriptive approach for developing the reading skills of community college students. Knox (1977) emphasizes the need to provide advance organizers and a clear structure for teaching and learning while relying on the abilities of the adult to learn for him/herself. Fincher (1976) reports research in support of small classes, sequential learning, some use of peer teaching, and a varying use of lecture and discussion to fit the situation. "The process of effective learning by adults varies with the content or the nature of the learning tasks" (Knox, 1976), (p. 97). Discussion and testing, films, and books provide the student with information. To acquire skill, the adult relies on simulation or coaching; role plays and discussions are the methods which yield attitude change.

Summary and Conclusions

A review of the literature on teacher effectiveness, time on task and attending behavior, teacher moves and methods, student characteristics, and adult learning contributes both to an understanding of important elements of the teaching process and an understanding of some next steps in research on teaching and learning. Much has been done but a great many more questions remain.

- Teacher Effectiveness

  The research on teacher effectiveness stresses the importance of the teacher in the teaching and learning process. Studies have tended to focus on elementary school teachers many of whom teach in low socio-economic status classrooms and many of whom are studied in the process of teaching reading or mathematics. The results of the research are in some cases tentative but they have begun to contribute to the knowledge of questioning, classroom management, grouping, class size, teacher directedness, praise, feedback, student involvement, teacher attitudes, and classroom climate.

- Time on Task and Attending Behavior

  Again, the majority of the studies of engaged time or academic learning time have been conducted in elementary classrooms during the teaching of reading or mathematics. In several cases the students are of low socio-economic status. Findings suggest that engaged time is related to achievement in the basic skills, but little research has been done with students of various backgrounds, in a range of subject matter, and beyond grade three. Time on task has been virtually unstudied with an adult population.

- Teacher Moves and Methods

  The research on teaching methods has been inconclusive and contradictory. Lecturing and discussion have been studied extensively and findings indicate that both methods are effective although their effectiveness may vary with the content, objectives, and complexity of the material being learned. Experiential methods have been less thoroughly examined, but available data suggest that this method is about as effective as those to which it has been compared. Secondary students and adults have comprised most of the populations studies. Several researchers conclude that a somewhat structured approach to teaching is most effective and that methods do vary in efficiency and in effect on student attitudes.

- Student Characteristics

One explanation for the inconclusive nature of the data on teaching methods is the assertion that students respond differently to different methods. Therefore, any given method can be effective with the student for whom it is well suited. Socio-economic status, cultural background, learning style and the nature of the subject matter all seem to influence student learning. Once again, the characteristics of elementary school students have been described in greater detail than have characteristics of adult learners.

- Adult Learning

The adult learner has been examined by both researchers and theorists who conclude that adults differ from one another in learning needs, styles, strategies, and preferences. Nonetheless, it appears to most of the adult educators that adults require learning that is self-directed, self-paced, relevant to personal or vocational interests, and participatory in nature. Adults expect to find learning rooted in their experiences and reliant on their abilities. A process design is favored over a content design, the educator provides a structure and the learner engages in study for him/herself. Accuracy and mastery are important to adults as are efficiency and effective use of time.

The evidence reveals some important behaviors for teachers of elementary students. In the early grades reading and mathematics achievement scores are related to time on task. However, student gains are affected by student background characteristics regardless of the teaching approach.

For adults the data are less informative. Teaching methods appear to be equivalent in producing achievement gains. Little has been done to examine teacher effects or time on task with an adult learner population. Student characteristics such as age, ethnicity, or cultural background have not been related to teacher effects or learner outcomes.

The study reported herein is an investigation of adult achievement in the cognitive domain and its relationship to time on task and teaching methods. The study constitutes a step toward understanding adults as learners and adults as teachers of other adults.

BIBLIOGRAPHY

Amster, H., et al. *Effectiveness of Schell's peer teaching program in mathematics for junior high school students.* Paper presented at the annual meeting of the American Educational Research Association, Washington, March 30 — April 3, 1975.

Armento, B. J. *Correlates of teacher effectiveness in social science concept instruction.* Paper presented at the annual meeting of the National Council for the Social Studies, Cincinnati, November 23-26, 1977.

Berliner, D. C. *The beginning teacher evaluation study: Overview and selected findings, 1975-1975.* Paper presented at the Conference on Teacher Effects: An Examination by Policy Makers and Researchers, Austin, November 2-4, 1975.

Berliner, D. C. Impediments to the study of teacher effectiveness. *Journal of Teacher Education,* 1976, 27, 5-13.

Berliner, D. C. and Gage, N. L. The psychology of teaching methods. In N. L. Gage (Ed.), *The Psychology of Teaching Methods — The Seventy-fifth Yearbook of the National Society for the Study of Education, Part I.* Chicago: The National Society for the Study of Education, 1976.

Berliner, D. C. and Rosenshine, B. *The acquisition of knowledge in the classroom.* Paper prepared for the Conference on Schooling and Educational Process, San Diego, November 20-22, 1975.

Beyer, B. K., et al. *History teaching project: A project to improve productivity in teaching at Carnegie-Mellon University through the development of self-paced instruction in undergraduate history,* Carnegie-Mellon University, 1975.

Blair, T. R. *Relationship of teacher effort and student achievement in reading,* University of Michigan, 1975.

Blair, T. R. Where to expend your teaching effort (it does count!). *Reading Teacher,* 1976, 30, 293-96.

Bligh, D. A pilot experiment to test the relative effectiveness of three kinds of teaching method. In *University Teaching Methods Unit.* London: London University, 1971.

Boracks, N. *Word recognition strategies of adult beginning readers.* Paper presented at the annual meeting of the Eastern Educational Research Association, Williamsburg, March, 1978.

Borg, W. R. Time and school learning. *Newsletter: Beginning Teacher Evaluation Study,* March, 1979, 2-7.

Brady, T. C. *A study in the application of the C. A. Curran counseling-learning model to adults,* Walden U., 1975.

Bravlio, A. I. *The cross cultural uses of educational methods and techniques with adults,* Indiana U., 1971.

Brophy, J. E. *Reflections on research in Elementary Schools.* Paper presented at the Conference on Teacher Effects: An Examination by Policy Makers and Researchers, Austin, November 2-4, 1975.

Brophy, J. E. and Evertson, C. M. *Teacher education, teacher effectiveness, and developmental psychology,* U. of Texas at Austin, August, 1975.

B.T.E.S.: An overview of selected themes. *Newsletter: Beginning Teacher Evaluation Study,* October, 1978, 1-4.

Coker, H. and Coker, J. G. *A competency based certification system.* Paper presented at the Conference on Teacher Effects: An Examination by Policy Makers and Researchers, Austin, November 2-4, 1975.

Collican, P. M. *Self-planned learning: Implications for the future of adult education,* Syracuse University Research Corporation, April, 1974.

Dauzat, S. V. *Louisiana adult performance level pilot study: A comparative analysis of APL Competency Based instructional programs,* Louisiana Tech U., 1978.

Donovan, M. A. and Austin, M. C. *Does modality preference make a difference? The results of a three-year study – empirical data.* Paper presented at the annual meeting of the International Reading Association, Houston, May 1-5, 1978.

Dubin, R. and Taveggia, T. C. *The teaching-learning paradox.* Eugene: Center for the Advanced Study of Educational Administration, 1968.

Elliott, P. H. *An exploratory study of adult learning styles,* 1975.

Even, M. J. *What we know about adult learning and what it means to the adult educator – with emphasis on learning in groups.* Paper presented to the Research Committee of the Adult Education Association, November 1, 1973.

Feringer, R. *The relations between learning problems of adults and general learning theory.* Speech presented to the Adult Education Research Conference, San Antonio, April 5-7, 1978.

Fincher, C. *What research says about learning.* Paper presented at Houston Baptist University, September 1, 1976.

Fitzmaurice, M. D. *Learning institute in-service results.* Paper presented at the Annual Meeting of the International Reading Association, Anaheim, May, 1976.

Forman, D. and Richardson, P. *The adult learner and educational television,* U. of Mid-America, 1976.

Fowler, C. W. As test scores have fallen, so has the time schools give to teaching. *American School Board Journal,* 1977, 164, 26+.

Frederick, Wayne C.; Walberg, Herbert; and Rasher, Sue Pinzur. Time, teacher comments and achievement in Urban high schools. *Journal of Educational Research,* 1979, 73, 63-65.

Gage, N. L.; Clark, C. M.; Marx, R. W.; Peterson, P. L.; Stayrook, N. G.; and Winne, P. H. *Preliminary Report of a factorially designed experiment on teacher structuring, soliciting, and reacting.* Paper presented at the Conference on Teacher Effects: An Examination by Policy Makers and Researchers, Austin, November 2-4, 1975.

Gagné, R. M. The learning basis of teaching methods. In N. L. Gage (Ed.), *The Psychology of Teaching Methods – The Seventy-fifth Yearbook of the National Society for the Study of Education, Part I.* Chicago: The National Society for the Study of Education, 1976.

Gall, M. D. and Gall, J. P. The discussion method. In N. L. Gage (Ed.), *The Psychology of Teaching Methods – The Seventy-fifth Yearbook of the National Society for the Study of Education, Part I.* Chicago: The National Society for the Study of Education, 1976.

Gelford, B., et al. An andragogical application to the training of social workers. *Journal of Education for Social Work,* 1975, 11, 55-61.

Hall, G. E. *The effects of "change" on teachers and professors – theory, research and implications for decision-makers.* Paper presented at the Conference on Teacher Effects: An Examination by Policy Makers and Researchers, Austin, November 2-4, 1975.

Harris, A. J. *The effective teacher of reading, revisited.* Paper presented to the International Reading Association Convention, Houston, May 3, 1978.

Hayson, J. History teaching: The issues approach and the classroom learning environment. *History and Social Science Teacher,* 1977, 12, 175-8.

Hollingsworth, C. D. *A comparison of verbal and nonverbal instruction in elementary school mathematics,* U. of Michigan, 1973.

Hoover, H. and Cauble, A. Concept versus expository method of teaching family relationships. *Home Economics Research Journal,* 1974, 3, 136-41.

Johnson, A. *Student success, student characteristics, and method of instruction: A summary of research and new findings,* Oklahoma State U., 1976.

Knowles, M. S. *The adult learner: A neglected species.* New York: Gulf Publishing, 1973.

Knowles, M. S. Andragogy not pedagogy. In S. M. Grabowski (Ed.), *Adult Learning and Instruction.* Washington, D. C., Adult Education Assoc., 1970.

Knowles, M. S. *Self-directed learning: A guide for learners and teachers.* New York: Association Press, 1975.

Knox, A. B. *Adult development and learning.* San Francisco: Jossey-Bass, 1977.

Knox, A. B. Helping adults to learn. In R. M. Smith (Ed.), *Adult Learning: Issues and Innovations,* ERIC, July, 1976.

Kreitlow, B. W. Innovation in organizing learning for adults. In R. M. Smith (Ed.), *Adult Learning: Issues and Innovations,* ERIC, July, 1976.

Kuhlman-Wilsdorf, D. Academic standards and grades. *Engineering Edu-Education,* 1975, 66, 160-64.

Leifer, A. D. Teaching with television and film. N. L. Gage (Ed.), *The Psychology of Teaching Methods — The Seventy-fifth Yearbook of the National Society for the Study of Education, Part I.* Chicago: The National Society for the Study of Education, 1976.

Long, Huey; McCrary, Kay; and Ackerman, Spencer. Adult Cognition: Piagetian based research findings. *Adult Education,* 1979, 30, 3-18.

McCannon, R. S. *Analysis of adult learning experiences in rural settings.* Paper presented at the Adult Education Research Conference, Minneapolis, April 21, 1977.

McCarney, S. B. and Bullock, L. M. Effects of differential instruction approaches upon undergraduate students. *The Journal of Educational Research,* 1977, 70, 6, 235-9.

McDonnald, F. J. *Research on teaching and its implications for policy making: Report on phase II of the beginning teacher evaluation study.* Paper presented at the Conference on Teacher Effects: An Examination by Policy Makers and Researchers, Austin, November 2-4, 1975.

McDonald, F. J. *Beginning teacher evaluation study, Phase II, 1973-74; Executive summary report.* Princeton: Educational Testing Service, 1976.

McDonald, J. B. Strategies of instruction in adult education. In S. M. Grabowski (Ed.), *Adult Learning and Instruction.* Washington, D.C.: Adult Education Assoc., 1970.

McKeachie, W. J. *Improving teaching effectiveness,* Office of Education, 1971.

McKeachie, W. J. Research on college teaching. *Educational Perspectives,* 1972, 11, 2, 3-10.

McLagan, P. A. *Behavior theory and adult education.* Paper presented at the Adult Education Research Conference, St. Louis, April, 1975.

McLeish, J. The lecture method. In N. L. Gage (Ed.), *The Psychology of Teaching Methods – The Seventy-fifth Yearbook of the National Society for the Study of Education, Part I.* Chicago: The National Society for the Study of Education, 1976.

Main, Keith. The power-load-margin formula of Howard Y. McClusky as the basis of a model of teaching. *Adult Education,* 1979, 30, 19-33.

Manzo, A. V. *Personality characterisics and learning style preferences of adult basic education students,* Missouri U., 1975.

Maxim, G. W. Effects of two instructional treatments on ability to interpret research. *Improving College and University Teaching,* 1977, 25, 108-109, 111.

Medley, D. M. *Teacher competence and teacher effectiveness,* AACTE, August, 1977.

Moore, M. G. Learner autonomy: The second dimension of independent learning. *Convergence,* 1972, 5, 76-88.

Moore, J. W. and Schaut, J. *An evaluation of the effects of conceptually appropriate feedback on teacher and student behavior,* Office of Education, 1975.

Murphy, P. D. *Strategies for college teaching.* Twenty-first annual faculty lecture, North Dakota State U., February 22, 1977.

Newman, H. J. *The comparative effectiveness of selected instructional strategies for the teaching of basic algebra,* U. of Michigan, 1974.

Oen, U. T. and Sweany, H. P. *The effectiveness of an individualized learning method of instruction when compared to the lecture-discussion method,* Michigan State U.,

Olander, H. T. and Robertson, H. C. The effectiveness of discovery and expository methods in the teaching of fourth-grade mathematics. *Journal of Research in Mathematics Education,* 1973, 4, 1, 33-44.

Olmstead, J. A. *Theory and state of the art of small group methods of instruction.* Alexandria, Va.: Human Resources Research Organization, March, 1970.

Overman, William. Effective communication – the key to student management. *NASSP Bulletin,* 1979, 63, 34-39.

Peck, R. F. *How do teachers and students interact to create the outcomes of education?* Paper presented at the Conference on Teacher Effects: An Examination by Policy Makers and Researchers, Austin, November 2-4, 1975.

Piaget, J. Development and learning. *Journal of Research in Science Teaching,* 1964, 2, 176-186.

Ramirez, A. G. *Teaching reading in Spanish: A study of teaching effectiveness,* Stanford U., March, 1978.

Reimanis, Gunars. *Teaching effectiveness and the interaction between teaching methods, student and teacher characteristics,* Corning Community Coll., 1972.

Rosenshine, B. *Short Review of Teaching Variables and Student Achievement.* Paper presented at the Conference on Teacher Effects: An Examination by Policy Makers and Researchers, Austin, November 2-4, 1975a.

Rosenshine, B. *Recent research on teaching behaviors and student achievement.* Paper presented at the Conference on Teacher Effects: An Examination by Policy Makers and Researchers. Austin, November 2-4, 1975b.

Rosenshine, B. *Recent research on teaching (Part II).* Paper presented at the Conference on Teacher Effects: An Examination by Policy Makers and Researchers, Austin, November 2-4, 1975c.

Rosenshine, B. Classroom instruction. In N. L. Gage (Ed.), *The Psychology of Teaching Methods – The Seventy-fifth Yearbook of the National Society for the Study of Education, Part I.* Chicago: The National Society for the Study of Education, 1976.

Rosenshine, B. V. and Berliner, D. C. *Academic engaged time.* Mimeographed.

Rouk, V. Separate studies show similar results of teacher effectiveness. In *Educational R and D Report,* 1979, 2, 6-10.

Sandefur, J. R. and Adams, R. A. *An evaluation of teaching: An interim research report.* Paper presented at the Conference on Teacher Effects: An Examination by Policy Makers and Researchers. Austin, November 2-4, 1975.

Schiavone, J. *A course in community college reading skills development for the adult learner,* City University of New York, 1978.

Schneider, E. Joseph. Degrees of Success while learning and academic achievement. *Education Digest,* January, 1980, 45, 21-3.

Segel, Robert A. What is good teaching? And why is there so little of it? *Chronicle of Higher Education,* September 24, 1979, 19, 21.

Seider, C. J. Teaching with simulations and games. In N. L. Gage (Ed.), *The Psychology of Teaching Methods – The Seventy-fifth Yearbook of the National Society for the Study of Education, Part I.* Chicago: The National Society for the Study of Education, 1976.

Shauelson, R. and Dempsey, N. *Generalizability of measures of teacher process. Beginning teacher evaluation study.* San Francisco: Far West Lab., 1975.

Smith, N. M. Allocation of time and achievement in elementary social studies. *The Journal of Educational Research*, 1979, 72, 231-36.

Soar, R. and Soar, R. Attempt to identify measures of teacher effectiveness from four studies. *Journal of Teacher Education,* November, 1974, 76, 261-7.

Stahl, R. J. *Innovation or renovation? Lecture, commentary, and discussion in the precollege psychology classroom.* Paper presented at the Annual Convention of the American Psychological Association, Washington, September, 1976.

Stallings, J. A. How instructional processes relate to child outcomes in a national study of follow through. *Journal of Teacher Education,* 1976, 27, 43-52.

Stallings, J. *A study of implementation in seven follow through educational models and how instructional processes relate to child outcomes.* Paper presented at the Conference on Teacher Effects: An Examination by Policy Maker and Researchers. Austin, November 2-4, 1975.

Stallings, J.; Needels, M.; and Stayrook, N. *How to change the process of teaching basic reading skills in secondary schools: Final report,* SRI International, May, 1979.

Tennyson, R. D. and Tennyson, C. L. *Content structure as a design strategy variable in concept acquisition.* Paper presented at the Annual Meeting of the American Educational Research Association, New York, April 4-8, 1977.

Thompson, J. R. Formal properties of instructional theory for adults. In S. M. Grabowski (Ed.), *Adult Learning and Instruction.* Washington, D.C.: Adult Education Assoc., 1970.

Ward, B. A. and Tikunoff, W. J. *Application of research to teaching.* Paper presented at the Conference on Teacher Effects: An Examination by Policy Makers and Researchers. Austin, November 2-4, 1975.

Warren, J. *A statistical analysis of the relative effectiveness of two methods of teaching general mathematics to twelfth grade students.* Bakersfield: Kern Joint Union High School District, Jan., 1973.

Weber, C. A comparison of values clarification and lecture methods in health education. *Journal of School Health,* May, 1978, 48, 269-74.

Weimer, R. C. *A critical analysis of the discovery versus expository research studies investigating retention or transfer within the areas of science, mathematics, vocational education, language and geography from 1908 to the present,* U. of Illinois at Urbana, 1974.

Widman, S. S. Adult learning. In S. S. Widman and S. G. Olswang (Eds.), *Proceedings: Conference on the Adult Learner.* Seattle: University of Washington, July, 1975.

Wilson, J. T. and Koran, J. J. *Review of research on mathemagenic behavior: implications for teaching and learning science,* Iowa University, September, 1975.

Chapter 4

PROBLEM ONE: A STUDY OF ADULT
ACHIEVEMENT IN RELATION TO
INSTRUCTIONAL TIME, METHOD,
AND COMPLEXITY OF CONCEPTS

- *W. Robert Houston*

A. TIME ON TASK

Background and Need

As the teacher population stabilizes in the United States, the need for more effective teacher education programs becomes more acute. Yet what is known about adult learning and instruction is meager. Some progress is being made in a number of related areas that have promise for teacher education.

In recent years, several researchers have explored the relationship between classroom practice and student achievement. (For summaries of their work, see Rosenshine, 1976; and Medley, 1977). Based on the twin assumptions that observation is the most valid procedure for adequately assessing instruction and that the basic purpose of instruction is to increase student achievement, these researchers have focused on teaching basic skills in the elementary and secondary schools. Two conclusions permeate these studies: (1) Time devoted to instruction is related to achievement, and (2) Instruction that is direct and controlled by the teacher is more effective. Three questions are pertinent for those concerned with teacher education. First, to what extent are these conclusions relevant for teaching adults? Medley (1977) noted that little data are available in teacher effects research beyond the third grade. While results have been extrapolated to older learners, little evidence supports this generalized conclusion. Houston, et al (1979) found no relation between time-on-task and adult achievement.

Second, to what extent are they relevant for content at higher cognitive levels such as analysis, synthesis, or application? Soar and Soar (1973) found that the proportion of pupils who appeared to be task-engaged was positively related to gain in simple − concrete learning outcomes, but negatively related to more complex learning outcomes.

Third, would results be similar in substantive areas other than the basic skills of reading and mathematics?

Fourth, studies of instructional time have not considered the potential curvilinear relation of time and achievement. In an analysis of this problem, Soar (1978) concluded that several studies (including Soar and Soar, 1973; Rim and Coller, 1978) found achievement gain "greatest where time on task was at an intermediate level, rather than either high or low level (p. 2)."

In addition to the teacher effects research, a number of studies have been conducted on teacher inservice education. The vast majority of these studies have relied on participant perception as the criterion of success. Satisfaction or the "happiness quotient" rather than change in cognitive achievement or practice has been employed as the basis for effectiveness. While a number of conclusions have been synthesized (Lawrence, 1974), the basis for their validity remains tenuous. What is needed are studies parallel in approach to those of the classroom effects research, but with adults as learners.

A third set of researchers have focused on adult learning in basic literacy and vocational competence. Experiential and process approaches have been found to be effective, a contrary finding to that for children. (Forman & Richardson 1976; Knowles, 1970; Houston et al., 1979). Process approaches or high cognitive concepts have seldom been part of adult-learning studies, and as yet research with adults "has not provided a firm basis . . . on which to base programs for adults (Forman & Richardson, 1976, p. 6)."

A vast array of studies have compared various instructional methods (e.g., lecture with television, lecture with discussion). "The overwhelming portion of these studies show few if any differences. (Murphy, 1977, p. 9)." Bligh (1971, p. 6) criticized these studies because few considered higher-level cognitive concepts. An examination of the procedures and data from several of these studies suggests that their power could be increased through analysis of variables such as time devoted to particular content and learner-attending behavior, use of direct observational techniques and content-specific achievement tests, and consideration of high and low cognitive concepts. As Gall and Gall (1976), concluded, "we do not think it fruitful to review the research once again to determine whether real differences between lecture and discussion exist. . . Instead, we recommend that efforts be turned to conducting new studies characterized by methodological rigor (p. 198).

These various sets of studies, conducted by researchers from different perspective, disciplines, and purposes, provide a basis for the study described herein. Summaries of salient research are included in Chapter 3. While their findings are not entirely consistent, they press those involved in the education of teachers to test several variables. These variables include time devoted to instruction, complexity and nature of concepts, and instructional method employed as each relates independently and in interaction with other variables to adult achievement.

Teacher education is too vital to be conducted without benefit of the most powerful research findings available. It is too important not to formulate studies which test hunches and validate findings from related studies. Without such a research base, the practice of teaching and teacher education will be limited in effectiveness.

In 1979, the authors of this report published a research study on adult learning. The study, reported in *Designing Short Term Instructional Programs* was based upon an analysis of the data collected for the evaluation of the 1977 CMTI. Several findings were unexpected.

(1) Achievement of a concept is not related to the amount of class time devoted to that concept.

(2) Adults in process-oriented groups achieve more than those in task-oriented groups. Those in groups that are not clearly task- or process-oriented achieve least.

The implications of these two findings upon adult populations are immense. First, the time-on-task result is in opposition to the research now being reported on learning characteristics of young children. It is logical to assume that adults and children will vary in their approach to learning, but prior studies have not reported this. To our knowledge, this CMTI report is the only study of adult learning where pre- and post-achievement test scores for 400 participants have been correlated with structured, daily observations.

The findings also raise major questions about the use of the lecture presentation mode as the best instructional approach for adults. This finding is consistent with many of the theorists in adult learning.

The study reported here is a refinement and adaption of the 1979 CMTI report. The observation instrument was restructured to provide more objective ways of categorizing process and task groups. Also, Donald Medley and Robert Soar assisted the authors prior to CMTI in designing the study and afterwards in analyzing the data.

A major question, addressed herein, is whether or not this study supports or refutes the findings on adult learning reported in the previous CMTI report.

Problem of the Study

The purpose of this study was to explore several variables that might have promise for improving the education of adults, particularly professionals such as teachers. The problem, posed as a question, was:

What is the relation between instructional time and
adult achievement, taking into consideration differences in content, complexity of concepts, and methods
of instruction?

Achievement was defined with reference to the complexity of concepts, and specifically, the dichotomous analysis
of lower cognitive concepts (knowledge and comprehension)
and higher cognitive concepts, such as analysis, synthesis, and
application (as per Bloom, 1956). Three content areas were
explored to test variations in content and to structure knowledge acquisition so as to include substantive areas other than
basic skills. The three content areas were: organizational
theory, multicultural concepts, and community education.
The first, study of organizations, was primarily cognitive in
content while the latter two areas involved cultural and
personal affective overtones. To summarize, achievement was
considered at two levels of cognition for three content areas.

Extensiveness of instructional time was defined as the observed instructional time devoted to the three content areas.
To study this concept more adequately, the instructional
methods employed were analyzed. Types of instruction in
each of the three substantive areas were classified as either (a)
presentation of low cognitive content, (b) presentation of
high cognitive content, (c) discussion, and (d) experiental
processes concerned with cognition. Two other methods of
instruction were studied that were not related specifically to
one of the three substantive areas" (e) experiental, non-
cognitive processes, and (f) non-instructional activities. These
fourteen methods of instruction (four methods for each of
three content areas plus two general methods) were considered both indivually and in logical combination.

B. PROCEDURES EMPLOYED IN STUDY

The intensive three-week institute described in Chapter 2
provided a basis for testing the major question of the study.
Common goals and resources provided a basis for examining
differences among the ten clusters.

Data were collected in several ways. Prior to and following CMTI, participants completed an achievement test to assess the basic concepts taught in the institute. Demographic data and perceptions of the institute were also collected from individual participants. In addition, each instructional cluster was observed regularly to describe the type and extensiveness of instruction.

This chapter is organized in four sections: development of achievement tests, collection and preparation of achievement data, collection and preparation of instructional time data, and data analysis.

Development of Achievement Tests

The achievement test was designed to reflect several features necessary for this study; (a) questions in the areas of organizational theory, multicultural education, and community study; (b) questions at both the high and low cognitive levels; (c) adequate number of questions for subscale reliability; and (d) content validity with respect to the general concepts of the institute. The content of the test was based on the objectives specified by the CMTI design team and content specialists, (See Appendix B), and the content of books and papers assigned for reading by students. To assure representativeness and test validity, each content objective was tested either at a high or low cognitive level, with a random draw to determine which level. A table of random numbers was employed to select other items for the test. After individual items were written, an independent audit was made to determine if questions had face validity with respect to both content and level of cognition.

The test was composed of 60 multiple-choice items. The six achievement scales and the number of test items in each are listed in Table 3. These generated five subtotals and a total test score.

Table 3: Achievement Test Scales and Number of Test Items

Achievement Scales	Number of Items
a. Organization, Higher Cognitive Levels Scale	10
b. Organization, Lower Cognitive Levels Scale	10
c. Multiculture, Higher Cognitive Levels Scale	10
d. Multiculture, Lower Cognitive Levels Scale	10
e. Community, Higher Cognitive Levels Scale	10
f. Community, Lower Cognitive Levels Scale	10
g. Organization, Subtotal	20
h. Multiculture, Subtotal	20
i. Community, Subtotal	20
j. Higher Cognitive Levels, Subtotal	30
k. Lower Cognitive Levels, Subtotal	30
l. Total	60

Achievement for each subject in the study was recorded for each of the twelve scales, subtotals, and total for the pretest and the posttest. Instrument reliability was tested using the Kuder-Richardson Split-Half Formula 21, with coefficients of .62 for the pretest and .60 for the posttest. Construct and content validity were based on the procedures employed in designing test items so as to reflect accurately the instructional program.

Collection and Preparation of Achievement Data

The 400 institute participants completed the 60-item pretest prior to attending CMTI and a parallel posttest at the end of the three-week institute. Demographic information was collected on the pretest to describe participants' personal characteristics. Participants assessed the effectiveness of the institute as part of the posttest. Copies of Pretests and posttests are found in Appendix A.

Data from the achievement tests were analyzed to determine if the dimensions of the test (content and level of cognition) were relatively independent. To assess this, the six achievement scales (a-f in Table 3) were used to generate five mutually orthogonal contrasts and a total achievement variable. These are arranged in Table 4.

Table 4: Orthogonal Contrasts Among Achievement Scales

Achievement Scales	Orthogonal Contrasts					
	A	B	C	D	E	F
Organization, Higher Cognitive Levels	+1	+1	+2	0	+2	0
Organization, Lower Cognitive Levels	+1	- 1	+2	0	- 2	0
Multiculture, Higher Cognitive Levels	+1	+1	- 1	+1	- 1	+1
Multiculture, Lower Cognitive Levels	+1	- 1	- 1	+1	+1	- 1
Community, Higher Cognitive Levels	+1	+1	- 1	- 1	- 1	- 1
Community, Lower Cognitive Levels	+1	- 1	- 1	- 1	+1	+1

*A - Total Achievement Dimension
 B - Higher Cognitive/Lower Cognitive Dimension
 C - Organization/Multiculture and Community Dimension
 D - Multiculture/Community Dimension
 E - Organization High Cognitive, Multiculture Low Cognitive, and Community Low Cognitive Dimension/Organization Low Cognitive, Multiculture High Cognitive and Community High Cognitive
 F - Multiculture High Cognitive and Community Low Cognitive/ Multiculture Low Cognitive and Community High Cognitive Dimension

The Total Achievement Dimension, A, was examined by a one-way analysis of variance to determine if significant differences existed among the six achievement scales. Had this test been nonsignificant, only A would have been employed in further analysis of achievement. Because it was significant at $p < .01$, the reliability of dimensions B-F was assayed. Those dimensions displaying reliability were tested using one-way analyses of variance to determine if significant differences were present within the five orthogonal contrasts. The results of these ANOVA are found in Table 5. All dimensions were statistically significant and those sub-scales could be used in analyses.

Using pretest and posttest data for the achievement scales of the study, regressed achievement measures were derived using the following procedure.

The process . . . consists of the following steps: (a) calculate the correlation between pretest and posttest; (5) predict each pupil's posttest on that basis; (c) subtract the

Table 5: *One-way ANOVA Results for 6 Orthogonal Contrasts for Residual Gain in Achievement*

Achievement Scales	F	P
A. Total achievement	1.91	.01
B. Hi/-Lo Cog	9.29	.01
C. Org & Mult/Com	575.14	.001
D. Mult/Com	180.17	.001
E. Org Hi & Mult Lo & Com Lo/Organ Lo & Mult Hi & Com Hi	150.97	.001
F. Mult Hi and Com Lo/Mult Lo and Com Hi	623.02	.001

predicted posttest from the actual posttest; and (d) use that difference score as the measure of gain for further analysis (Soar, 1978)

These residual scores for significant dimensions of the test were employed as measures of achievement in the study.

Collection and Preparation of Instructional Time Data

The extensiveness of instructional time was determined through structured observations of clusters. A sign-based observation system was used to collect these data (see Appendix C for a copy of the observation instrument and Observation Guide). Each of the ten clusters was observed for at least three twenty-minute periods each day for a total of fifty twenty-minute periods during CMTI. Observation times and observers were assigned so as to ensure that each cluster was observed an equal number of times by each observer.

Two-minutes segments formed the basic unit for observation; thus, ten units or segments were observed during each twenty-minute period. Each of the ten clusters was observed in 500 two-minutes segments during CMTI.

Observers recorded incidence of fourteen instructional methods during each segment. The proportion of each twenty-minutes observation that was devoted to each of the fourteen instructional methods was as a basic unit for determining instructional time. These data, pooled for each measure and each cluster, provided the basis for describing the extent and nature of instruction. The fourteen instructional methods are listed in Table 6.

Table 6: *Categories of Instructional Method Observed*

Organization
1. Present-high cognitive
2. Present-low cognitive
3. Discussion-cognitive
4. Experiential-cognitive

Multiculture
5. Present-high cognitive
6. Present-low cognitive
7. Discussion-cognitive
8. Experiential-cognitive

Community
9. Present-high cognitive
10. Present-low cognitive
11. Discussion-cognitive
12. Experiential-cognitive

13. Experiential non-cognitive
14. Non-instructional

Each of these classes of instructional methods is defined in the following paragraphs.

1. *Presentation of content at lower cognitive levels.* Instruction may be lecture, audio-visual, demonstration, or other method but is primarily expository and concerned with direct instruction related either to multicultural education, community education or organizational theory. The instructors will typically be responsible; however, participants could be giving information or instruction. Learners may occasionally ask questions, but these primarily are clarifying questions seeking clarifying answers. The level of cognition is either knowledge or comprehension, when defined, using Bloom's Taxonomy.

2. *Presentation of content at higher cognitive levels.* The same rules as above apply except that cognitive levels

are higher, involving analysis, synthesis, application, or evaluation.

3. *Discussion.* Learners are engaged in discussion of substantive issues related either to multicultural education, community, or organizational theory. They may be in several groups in the room. Speakers are primarily students; interaction is open. Instructors may be involved in the discussion but not central figures providing new data.

4. *Experiential-cognitive process.* Simulation, intellectual games, and role playing are illustrations of experiential activities. The emphasis is on *experiencing* rather than *talking about* (discussion). In this factor, the experience must clearly relate either to increased understanding or appreciation of organizational concepts or multicultural education, or the relationship must be strongly inferred.

5. *Experiential non-cognitive process.* This includes experiences where the objectives are not related to increasing understanding of CMTI concepts. Activities include get-acquainted exercises, self-development role playing, *non-cognitive* physical activities designed for group building or group health.

6. *Non-instructional activities.* This includes periods of transition between activities, breaks for lunch or coffee/juice, administrative tasks, housekeeping activities, and announcements. Their general characteristic is maintenance of the organization or periods of confusion.

It could be anticipated that some of these fourteen factors would be more variable than others. In that case, they would have extended a greater influence on the results of subsequent analyses; therefore, raw observation measures were standardized and normalized.

While careful attention had been paid to balanced assignment of observers to clusters, and to random selection of the
times each observation was to occur, systematic errors attributable to observer bias might have occurred. To test for this, a
two-way analysis of variance was calculated using cluster (C)
and observers (0) as independent variables, with the interaction C X 0 indicating any observer bias that affected cluster
data.

Further analyses of observation data were made to determine if the dimensions of the instrument were relatively independent. To assess this, the fourteen categories listed in
Table 4 were employed to generate thirteen mutually orthogonal contrasts. These are arranged in Table 7.

Table 7: *Orthogonal Contrasts Among Observational Scales*

Instructional Content and Method	Level of Cognition	Orthogonal Contrasts*												
		A	B	C	D	E	F	G	H	I	J	K	L	M
Organization														
1. Presentation	High	+1	+1	+2	0	+2	0	-7	0	0	0	0	0	0
2. Presentation	Low	+1	-1	+2	0	-2	0	-7	0	0	0	0	0	0
3. Discussion		+1	0	+2	0	0	0	+6	-1	+1	+2	+2	0	0
4. Experiential	Cognitive	+1	0	+2	0	0	0	+6	-1	-1	+2	-2	0	0
Multiculture														
5. Presentation	High	+1	+1	-1	+1	-1	+1	-7	0	0	0	0	0	0
6. Presentation	Low	+1	-1	-1	+1	+1	-1	-7	0	0	0	0	0	0
7. Discussion		+1	0	-1	+1	0	0	+6	-1	+1	-1	-1	+1	+1
8. Experiential	Cognitive	+1	0	-1	+1	0	0	+6	-1	-1	-1	+1	+1	-1
Community														
9. Presentation	High	+1	+1	-1	-1	-1	-1	-7	0	0	0	0	0	0
10. Presentation	Low	+1	-1	-1	-1	+1	+1	-7	0	0	0	0	0	0
11. Discussion		+1	0	-1	-1	0	0	+6	-1	+1	-1	-1	-1	-1
12. Experiential	Cognitive	+1	0	-1	-1	0	0	+6	-1	-1	-1	+1	-1	+1
13. Experiential	Non-Cognitive	+1	0	0	0	0	0	+6	+6	0	0	0		0
14. Non-Instructional		-13	0	0	0	0	0	0	0	0	0	0		0

Orthogonal Contrasts (Table 7)*

    A.* Instructional/Non Instructional
    B. Presentation High Cognitive/Present Low Cognitive
    C. Organization/Multiculture and Community
    D. Multiculture/Community

E. (High Cognitive/Low Cognitive) X (Organization/Multiculture and Community)
F. (High Cognitive/Low Cognitive) X (Multiculture/Community)
G. Presentation/Interactive Instruction
H. Cognitive Interactive/Non-Cognitive Interactive
I. Discussion Cognitive/Experiential Cognitive
J. Organization Cognitive Interactive/Multiculture and Community Cognitive Interactive
K. (Discussion/Experiential Cognitive) X (Organization/Multiculture and Community)
L. Multiculture Cognitive Interactive/Community Cognitive Interactive
M. (Discussion/Experiential Cognitive) X (Multiculture/Community)

One-way analyses of variance were calculated for each of the thirteen contrasts to determine if differences in each were significant. Those contrasts yielding significant differences were used in the analyses of the hypotheses of the study. Table 8 summarizes the results of these analyses.

Table 8: *One-way ANOVA Results for 13 Orthogonal Contrasts in Observation Instrument*

Variable		F	P	Accepted
A.	Instru vs. Non Instru.	11.90	.001	*
B.	Present Hi vs. Lo Cog.	227.73	.001	*
C.	Org. vs. Mult. & Com.	10.62	.001	*
D.	Mult. vs. Com.	68.23	.001	*
E.	Hi and Low Cog. vs. Organ./Mult & Com.	.19	.66	
F.	Hi and Low Cog. vs. Mult & Com.	79.68	.001	*
G.	Present vs. Interaction	17.89	.001	*
H.	Cog. Inter. vs. Non-cog. Inter.	.07	.79	
I.	Dis. Cog. vs. Exp. Cog.	55.57	.001	*
J.	Org. Cog. Int. vs. Mult. and Com. Cog. Int.	.98	.55	
K.	Dis/Exp/Cog. vs. Org/Mult/Com.	1.19	.11	
L.	Mult. Cog. Int. vs. Com. Cog. Int.	1.09	.27	
M.	Dis/Exp/Cog. vs. Mult/Com.	.13	.57	

Seven of the 13 contrasts were significant. These are marked with an * in Table 8.

C. ANALYSIS OF DATA

The problem of this study, stated as a null hypothesis was:

There is no relation between time devoted to instruction of adults and their achievement, taking into consideration differences in content, level of cognition, and methods of instruction.

Data related to this problem are presented in three sections. In the first section, achievement of adult learners is reported for different content areas and at different levels of cognition. The second section reports data related to time devoted to various instructional methods in each content area. Finally, achievement is analyzed with respect to time devoted to instruction.

Participant Achievement

Participants studied three content areas in CMTI: Community, Education that is Multicultural, and Organizational Theory. Their achievement on these content areas was measured for high and low cognitive levels. Raw pretest and posttest data for each of the subscales are reported in Table 9.

Table 9: Means and Standard Deviations for Achievement Test Sub-scales on Pre- and Posttest (n=386)

Achievement	Posttest		Pretest				
	X̄	S.D.	X̄	S.D.	Change	t	p
Community	13.65	2.45	10.32	2.62	3.33	18.21	.001
High Cognitive	6.46	1.69	4.64	1.65	1.82	15.13	.001
Low Cognitive	7.18	1.30	5.67	1.62	1.51	14.29	.001
Multiculture	14.00	1.91	10.60	2.26	3.40	22.55	.001
High Cognitive	7.32	1.37	4.68	1.64	2.64	17.44	.001
Low Cognitive	6.68	1.04	5.91	1.29	.77	9.13	.001
Organization	12.95	2.74	10.93	2.64	2.02	10.42	.001
High Cognitive	5.85	1.72	4.90	1.64	.95	7.85	.001
Low Cognitive	7.09	1.62	6.03	1.66	1.06	8.98	.001
High Cognitive	19.63	3.51	14.23	3.50	5.40	67.52	.001
Low Cognitive	20.96	2.96	17.61	3.43	3.35	14.49	.001
Total	40.60	5.69	31.84	5.99	8.76	20.72	.001

All changes in achievement were positive and statistically significant. From these data it can be concluded that participants gained in achievement during CMTI. Low cognitive scores were generally higher than high cognitive scores; however, the greatest gain was in high cognitive scores.

Based on Soar's recommendations (1978), each partici- pant's raw scores were converted to residual scores to elimi- nate intervening factors such as test ceiling effects. Sub- scale and scale scores were independently computed, thus leading to different regression weights and intercepts. Sums of subscales are not equal to scale scores for residual scores because each is independently computed. Table 10 in- cludes residuals for each cluster and each subscale and scale score.

Table 10: Residual Gains in Achievement by Clusters for High and Low Cognition in Community, Multicultural, and Organizational Concepts

Residual Achievement	Cluster*										
	A	B	C	D	E	F	G	H	I	J	Total
Community	6.92	8.02	7.53	7.24	7.21	7.07	6.86	7.81	6.76	6.74	7.22
High Cognitive	3.21	4.21	3.52	3.79	3.60	3.84	3.58	3.88	3.72	3.24	3.66
Low Cognitive	1.81	1.99	2.18	1.76	1.81	1.40	1.52	2.08	1.26	1.64	1.77
Multiculture	4.88	5.42	5.49	4.77	5.56	4.35	5.07	6.48	5.24	5.27	5.26
High Cognitive	1.32	1.46	1.32	0.85	1.68	0.95	0.96	1.75	1.51	1.11	1.29
Low Cognitive	2.09	2.42	2.61	2.40	2.39	1.89	2.63	3.21	2.23	2.68	2.46
Organization	11.00	12.53	11.41	10.04	10.71	11.91	11.82	12.22	11.07	12.14	11.50
High Cognitive	3.28	3.77	3.11	2.68	3.25	3.47	3.28	3.67	3.53	3.47	3.35
Low Cognitive	4.21	5.10	4.73	3.80	4.05	4.93	4.94	5.01	3.95	5.07	4.59
High Cognitive	12.24	14.18	12.62	11.95	12.96	12.82	12.28	13.89	13.32	12.28	12.86
Low Cognitive	12.97	14.30	14.40	12.64	12.99	13.03	13.86	15.16	12.20	14.22	13.60
Total	33.01	36.38	34.95	32.36	33.59	33.61	33.95	36.88	33.30	34.30	34.26

When scores were translated to residuals, low cognitive concepts were slightly, but not significantly, higher than high cognitive scores (mean of 13.60 compared with 12.86). Organizational theory concepts showed the greatest gain, followed by community, then multicultural education.

Table 11 includes ranks for each cluster for each scale and sub-scale, providing another perspective of residual achieve- ment.

*These letters do not correspond to the actual cluster numbers. They have been mixed in order to preserve the privacy of each of the clusters.

Table 11: Ranks by Cluster for Residual Gains in Achievement (10=High; 1=Low)

Residual Achievement	Cluster									
	A	B	C	D	E	F	G	H	I	J
Community	4.0	10.0	8.0	7.0	6.0	5.0	3.0	9.0	2.0	1.0
High Cognitive	1.0	10.0	3.0	7.0	5.0	8.0	4.0	9.0	6.0	2.0
Low Cognitive	6.5	8.0	10.0	5.0	6.5	2.0	3.0	9.0	1.0	4.0
Multiculture	3.0	7.0	8.0	2.0	9.0	1.0	4.0	10.0	5.0	6.0
High Cognitive	5.5	7.0	5.5	1.0	9.0	2.0	3.0	10.0	8.0	4.0
Low Cognitive	2.0	6.0	7.0	5.0	4.0	1.0	8.0	10.0	3.0	9.0
Organization	3.0	10.0	5.0	1.0	2.0	7.0	6.0	9.0	4.0	8.0
High Cognitive	4.5	10.0	2.0	1.0	3.0	6.5	4.5	9.0	8.0	6.5
Low Cognitive	4.0	10.0	5.0	1.0	3.0	6.0	7.0	8.0	2.0	9.0
High Cognitive	2.0	10.0	5.0	1.0	7.0	6.0	3.5	9.0	8.0	3.5
Low Cognitive	3.0	8.0	9.0	2.0	4.0	5.0	6.0	10.0	1.0	7.0
Total	2.0	9.0	8.0	1.0	5.0	4.0	6.0	10.0	3.0	7.0

Clusters were ranked according to their residual achievement gain. The cluster ranked 10 demonstrated the greatest residual gain for that particular scale or sub-scale. Based on these ratings, Cluster H achieved the highest residual achievement, followed by Cluster B. Cluster B's somewhat lower rank for multicultural achievement seemed to be the major difference between the two.

Cluster D demonstrated the lowest total achievement, even though it ranked 7 for community study. Other clusters with generally low achievement were A and I.

Instructional Methods

A number of instructional methods were employed by instructors in CMTI. These are presented in Table 12 and summarized by categories in Table 13.

When considering all Clusters as a group, organization and multiculture concepts were the basis for instruction to a greater extent than community concepts (33.30 and 35.54 percents as compared with 13.65 percent of the time). A total of 82.50 percent of CMTI was devoted to presentations, discussions, and experiential activities related to these three concepts.

Presentations accounted for nearly half the time 47.62 percent), with the majority of these concerned with high-

Table 12: Percent of Time Each Cluster Observed Engaging in Instructional Activities

Instructional Method	Cluster										All Clusters
	A	B	C	D	E	F	G	H	I	J	
Community											
Present Lo Cog	0.40	2.56	4.28	6.96	5.03	2.04	0.78	4.65	0.00	2.04	2.87
Present Hi Cog	3.10	5.62	4.30	0.80	10.50	5.20	4.72	9.26	2.68	2.52	4.87
Discuss Cog	3.03	4.34	4.01	3.57	7.12	6.09	3.26	7.35	4.04	1.63	4.44
Experiental Cog	0.00	1.75	2.08	0.67	1.80	3.46	2.12	0.00	2.32	0.60	1.48
Multiculture											
Present Lo Cog	0.91	1.42	3.59	2.97	2.81	0.35	3.69	4.02	3.90	5.26	2.89
Present Hi Cog	23.12	23.68	18.41	18.36	17.69	10.54	22.73	18.98	29.95	15.17	19.86
Discuss Cog	7.86	8.91	4.78	9.04	6.06	8.67	6.05	11.89	10.89	7.82	8.20
Experiental Cog	9.11	5.54	5.30	7.31	0.44	4.27	0.69	2.12	5.94	5.14	4.59
Organization											
Present Lo Cog	3.74	3.75	4.17	6.59	2.91	5.96	5.22	3.07	3.18	2.58	4.12
Present Hi Cog	12.40	13.41	17.07	14.95	18.93	9.99	12.34	6.55	7.25	17.21	13.01
Discuss Cog	11.40	9.92	6.97	8.11	6.12	12.80	6.90	6.82	4.82	10.89	8.48
Experiental Cog	6.66	9.23	4.86	6.48	3.92	10.74	13.74	9.88	2.57	8.94	7.70
Experiental Non-Cog	9.00	1.77	9.84	2.50	2.85	3.13	9.07	5.28	9.52	8.01	6.10
Non- instructional	9.27	8.11	8.40	9.81	9.89	14.83	6.74	10.11	12.94	8.27	9.84
Total percent of observations	100	100	98	98	96	98	98	100	100	96	99

cognitive concepts (37.74 percent of time) while low cognitive-based presentations were observed 9.88 percent of time. During about one-fifth (21.12) percent) of CMTI, discussions were conducted. Cognitively-based experiences dealing with one or more of the three concepts were conducted 13.77 percent while non-cognitive experiential activities accounted for 6.10 percent of the time. Non-instructional activities such as transitions, announcements, organizational tasks, and movement between activities accounted for nearly percent of the time (9.84 percent).

Clusters varied widely in the amount of time devoted to particular concepts and/or instructional methods. For example, the range for organizational concepts was from 17.84 percent for Cluster I to 39.62 percent for Cluster J. With multicultural concepts the range was from 23.83 to 50.69. For community study, the range was from 6.53 to 24.45.

Table 13: Summary of Percent of Time Each Cluster Observed Engaging in
Instructional Activities

Instructional Variable	Cluster										All Clusters
	A	B	C	D	E	F	G	H	I	J	
Community, Total	6.53	14.27	14.67	12.00	24.45	16.79	10.88	21.26	9.04	6.79	13.66
Multiculture, Total	41.00	39.55	32.08	37.68	27.00	23.83	33.16	37.01	50.69	33.39	35.54
Organization, Total	34.20	36.31	33.07	36.11	31.88	39.49	38.20	26.32	17.84	39.62	33.30
Presentation, Total	35.01	50.44	51.82	50.61	57.87	34.08	49.48	46.53	46.96	44.78	47.62
Presentation, Hi Cog	29.96	42.71	39.78	34.11	47.12	25.73	39.79	34.79	39.88	34.90	37.74
Presentation, Lo Cog	5.05	7.73	12.04	16.50	10.75	8.35	9.69	11.74	7.08	9.88	9.88
Experiental, Lo Cog	15.77	16.52	12.24	14.46	6.16	18.47	16.55	12.00	10.83	14.68	13.77
Discussion, Cog	22.29	23.17	15.76	20.72	19.30	27.56	16.21	26.06	19.75	20.34	21.12
Experiental Non-Cog	9.00	1.77	9.84	2.50	2.85	3.13	9.07	5.28	9.52	8.01	6.10
Non-Instructional	9.27	8.11	8.40	9.81	9.89	14.83	6.74	10.11	12.94	8.27	9.84

Cluster F presented material only 34.08 percent of the time while Cluster E presented information 57.87 percent of CMTI. Experiental activities dealing with cognitive concepts ranged from 6.16 to 18.47 percent of CMTI while non-cognitive experiential activities ranged from 1.77 percent to 9.52 percent of the time.

Differences in instructional patterns among clusters provided a basis for examining the relationship between amount and type of instruction and participant achievement. This relationship is explored in the following section.

Achievement and Time Devoted to Instruction

The basic question of this study was concerned with the relation between achievement of high and low cognitive concepts and instructional time and method devoted to those concepts. Differences in cluster achievement and instructional methods, outlined in the previous two sections, provide the basis for this analysis.

Because observations were based on ten clusters, the analyses were necessarily limited to an n of 10 even though these represented nearly 400 participants. Because of this, a number of comparisons were made to determine if any supported the thesis that time devoted to instruction was related to achievement. Table 14 includes correlation coefficients between instructional method and time and participant residual achievement. Because of the small n, the Spearman Rho correlation method was employed in these calculations.

Of the 240 correlations only 19 were statistically significant at $p < .05$. This was slightly more than could be expected by chance if all were considered; however, many were not conceptually related and should not be considered. Significant correlations are listed below because of their interesting pattern.

Presenting low cognitive on a particular content was significantly related to achievement in that area for two areas (multiculture and community), but not in organization. Presenting high cognitive on a particular content was significantly related to achievement in that area only in organization, although the other two coefficients were positive (.13 and .30). Total achievement in community and in multiculture were related to the instructional time devoted to low cognitive presentations in that area. Achievement in multiculture was negatively related to achievement in organizational theory. Non-cognitive experiential activities were consistently (but not significantly) negatively related to achievement of all areas.

Finally, Table 16 compares the time allocations of the five highest achieving clusters and the five lowest achieving clusters. (Based upon Table 13.)

While our analysis did not report significant difference between or among the clusters, certain patterns are interesting. In five areas, the time spent was within two points. However, in four areas, the highest achieving clusters spent more time:

Organization, Total	(+17)
Presentation, Total	(+17)

Table 14: Correlation Between Achievement Residuals and Instructional Time (n=10)

Achievement Residual	Community					Multiculture					Organization					E		Presentation		
	P-L	P-H	D	EC	TOT	P-L	P-H	D	EC	TOT	P-L	P-H	D	EC	TOT	N-C	N-I	TOT	P-H	P-L
Community	.64	.60	.30	.05	.65	-.04	.01	-.03	-.07	-.07	.02	.03	-.06	-.04	-.26	-.47	-.36	.43	.09	.39
High Cognitive	.33	.31	.25	.54	.58	-.29	.14	.20	-.01	.03	.38	-.27	-.06	.19	-.13	-.41	-.08	.08	.10	.10
Low Cognitive	.66	.54	.18	-.39	.39	.22	-.07	-.25	-.06	-.05	-.26	.37	-.09	-.23	-.28	-.32	-.46	.42	.12	.42
Multiculture	.59	.73	.41	-.52	.48	.73	.18	.13	-.50	-.08	-.64	-.19	-.48	.44	-.50	-.25	.01	.47	.60	.32
High Cognitive	.41	.77	.60	-.42	.35	.48	.30	.33	-.41	.23	-.65	-.19	-.31	-.60	-.93	-.22	.20	.21	.54	-.12
Low Cognitive	.52	.46	.13	-.47	.08	.73	.03	-.06	-.44	-.01	-.44	-.15	-.45	-.16	.07	-.20	-.13	.21	.22	.52
Organization	.01	.28	.00	.25	.12	.13	-.28	-.17	-.42	-.05	-.25	.45	.06	.33	.33	.00	.22	-.37	.04	-.18
High Cognitive	-.08	.39	.24	.13	-.01	.13	.00	.24	-.40	.35	-.40	.65	.04	.07	.06	-.06	.10	-.46	.15	-.52
Low Cognitive	.12	.24	-.06	.27	.04	.12	-.47	-.40	-.43	-.14	-.13	-.24	.11	.43	.49	-.02	-.34	-.30	.08	-.14
High Cognitive	.31	.62	.44	.14	.53	.11	.20	.32	-.30	.04	-.26	-.48	-.17	-.15	-.39	-.29	.04	.10	.52	-.19
Low Cognitive	.47	.49	.07	-.18	.39	.43	-.28	-.34	-.44	-.35	-.35	-.08	-.14	.09	.15	-.17	-.38	.04	.07	.33
Total	.46	.63	.24	-.04	.41	.34	.07	-.07	-.42	-.22	-.37	-.31	-.19	-.01	.01	-.23	-.25	.13	.35	.21

KEY: P-L = Presentation – Low Cognitive   P-H = Presentation – High Cognitive   D = Discussion
       EC = Experiental Cognitive   E N-C = Experiental Non-Cognitive   N-I = Non-Instructional
       TOT = Total

Boxed correlation coefficients were significant at $p < .05$ or greater.

Table 14a: Listing of Significant Correlations in Table 14

	Achievement Variable	Instructional Variable	Direction of Correlation
1.	Community, Total	Total Instruction, Community	Positive
2.	Community, Total	Present Low Cog, Community	Positive
3.	Community, Total	Present High Cog, Community	Positive
4.	Community, High Cognitive	Total Instruction, Community	Positive
5.	Community, Low Cognitive	Present Low Cog, Community	Positive
6.	Multiculture, Total	Present Low Cog, Multiculture	Positive
7.	Multiculture, Total	Present Low Cog, Community	Positive
8.	Multiculture, Total	Present High Cog, Total	Positive
9.	Multiculture, Total	Present High Cog, Community	Positive
10.	Multiculture, Total	Total Instruction, Community	Negative
11.	Multiculture, Total	Present Low Cog, Organization	Negative
12.	Multiculture, High Cognitive	Present Low Cog, Organization	Positive
13.	Multiculture, High Cognitive	Experiental Cog Activities Org.	Positive
14.	Multiculture, High Cognitive	Present High Cog, Community	Positive
15.	Multiculture, High Cognitive	Present Low Cog, Community	Positive
16.	Multiculture, Low Cognitive	Present Low Cog, Multiculture	Positive
17.	Organization, High Cognitive	Present High Cog, Organization	Positive
18.	High Cognitive, Total	Present High Cog, Community	Positive
19.	Total Achievement	Present High Cog, Community	Positive

Presentation, High Cognitive   (+18)
Experiental Cognitive   (+11)

In one area the highest achieving clusters spent less time:

Non-instruction   (−15)

The pattern appears clear. Higher achieving clusters spent more time in presentations and in experiential activities and less time in non-instructional activities.

Table 15

	High Cluster						Low Cluster						
	H	B	C	J	G	Total	D	A	I	F	E	Total	Difference
Community, Total	21.26	14.27	14.27	6.79	10.88	67.52	12.00	6.53	9.04	16.79	24.45	68.87	- 1
Multiculture, Total	37.01	39.55	39.55	33.39	33.16	182.66	37.68	41.00	50.69	23.83	27.00	180.20	- 2
Organization, Total	26.32	36.31	36.31	39.62	38.20	176.76	36.11	34.20	17.84	39.49	31.88	159.32	+17
Presentation, Total	46.53	50.44	50.44	44.78	49.48	241.67	50.61	35.01	46.96	34.08	57.87	224.53	+17
Presentation, Hi Cog	34.79	42.71	42.71	34.90	39.79	194.90	34.11	29.96	39.88	25.73	47.12	176.00	+18
Presentation, Lo Cog	11.74	7.73	7.73	9.88	9.69	46.77	16.50	5.05	7.08	8.35	10.75	47.73	- 1
Experiental, Cog	12.00	16.52	16.52	14.68	16.55	76.28	14.46	15.77	10.83	18.47	6.16	65.69	+11
Discussion, Cog	26.06	23.17	23.17	20.34	16.21	108.95	20.72	22.29	19.75	27.56	19.30	109.62	- 1
Experiental, Non-Cog	5.28	1.77	1.77	8.01	9.07	25.90	2.50	9.00	9.52	3.13	2.85	27.00	- 2
Non-Instructional	10.11	8.11	8.11	8.27	6.74	41.34	9.81	9.27	12.94	14.83	9.89	56.74	- 15

References

Bligh, D. A pilot experiment to test the relative effectiveness of three kinds of teaching methods. In *University Teaching Methods Unit*. London: London University, 1971.

Bloom, B. S., Engelhart, M. D., Furst, E. J., Hill, W. H. and Krathwohl, D. R. (eds.). *Taxonomy of educational objectives: the classification of education goals, handbook 1: cognitive domain*. New York: David McKay, 1956.

Fincher, C. *What research says about learning*. Paper presented at Houston Baptist University, Houston, September 1, 1976.

Forman, D. & Richardson, P. *The adult learner and educational television*. Lincoln, Neb: University of Mid-America, 1976.

Gall, M. D. & Gall, J. P. *The discussion method*. In N. L. Gage (Ed.), *The psychology of teaching methods: the 75th yearbook* of the National Society for the Study of Education, Part 1. Chicago: University of Chicago Press, 1976.

Houston, W. R., Andrews, T. E., and Bryant, B. Empirical study of institute strategies in F. T. Waterman, et al. *Designing Short-term Instructional Programs*. Washington, D. C.: Association of Teacher Educators, 1979, pp 87-146.

Knowles, M. S. *The adult learner: a neglected species*. New York: Gulf Publishing, 1973.

Lawrence, G. *Patterns of effective inservice education*. Tallahassee: Florida Department of Education, 1974.

Medley, D. M. *Teacher competence and teacher effectiveness*. Washington, D. C.: American Association of Colleges for Teacher Education, 1977.

Murphy, P. D. *Strategies for college teaching*. Twenty-first annual faculty lecture, North Dakota State University, February 22, 1977.

Rosenshine, B. Classroom instruction. In N. L. Gage (Ed.), *The psychology of teaching methods: the 75th yearbook of the National Society for the Study of Education*, Part 1. Chicago: University of Chicago Press, 1976.

Soar, R. S. Comments on time on task. Mimeo. Gainesville, Florida: College of Education, University of Florida, 1978.

Soar, R. S. & Soar, R. M. *Classroom behavior, pupil characteristics, and pupil growth for the school year and the summer*. Gainesville: Institute for Development of Human Resources, College of Education, University of Florida, 1973.

Chapter 5

PROBLEM TWO: A STUDY OF ATTITUDE, PERSONAL CHARACTERISTICS, AND ACHIEVEMENT

- *W. Robert Houston*

In discussions relating to the first study reported herein, the issue of attitudes of participants continued to surface. Certain clusters appeared to exhibit more positive attitudes toward the institute, its goals, its activities, and its instruction. Two questions were posed which formed the basis for this second study.
1. Were any differences in attitude among clusters related to achievement in those clusters?
2. Was there a relation between (a) achievement and (b) attitude and personal characteristics among individual participants?

A. DATA COLLECTION AND ANALYSIS

Data required to answer these two questions were drawn from three sources: pretest and posttest achievement scores of individual participants, personal characteristics elicited as part of the pretest, and attitude toward the institute. The instrumentation and results for achievement and personal characteristics have previously been described. The attitude scale is discussed in the following paragraphs.

At the end of the institute, participants rated 27 statements to express their feelings about CMTI. These items, numbered

60-87, were included with the posttest. They represented nine scales.

Table 16: Items Contributing to Attitude Scales

Scale	Item Numbers Contributing to Scale
General Attitude	61, 70, 79
Faculty	62, 71, 80
Content	63, 72, 81
Organization	64, 73, 82
Instruction	65, 74, 83
Multicultural Study	66, 75, 84
Organizational Study	67, 76, 85
Community Study	68, 77, 86
Instructional Analysis	69, 78, 87

Participants reacted to each of the 27 items on a 5-point scale: 1-Strongly Disagree; 2-Disagree; 3-Neutral; 4-Agree; 5-Strongly Agree. Some items were negatively stated; this was accounted for in the scoring process so that positive pre-ceptions consistently were scored with 5 as high and 1 as low.

The first scale was composed of items expressing general satisfaction with the institute. The next four scales probed perceptions of the faculty, the content or substance taught in the institute, the organization of CMTI, and the instructional strategies used. The last four scales were concerned with the actual content included in the institute: the study of cultures in a multicultural society, the study of organizations, the study of the community, and the analysis of instruction. The mean rating of the 386 participants completing the posttest for each of these nine scales is included in Table 17.

Table 17: Means and Standard Deviation for Nine Attitude Scales (n=386)

Variable	M	S.D.
General Attitude	3.94	.86
Faculty	3.98	.80
Content	3.51	.78
Organization	3.19	.81
Instruction	3.63	.59
Multicultural Study	3.84	.83
Organizational Study	3.69	.79
Community Study	3.80	.72
Instructional Analysis	3.41	.72
TOTAL	3.66	.59

The highest rating was accorded faculty, followed closely by items expressing general satisfaction with the institute. The lowest rated scale was related to the organization of the institute. When the four content areas were considered, multicultural study and community study were rated higher than organization study with instructional analysis lowest.

B. ATTITUDE AND ACHIEVEMENT BY CLUSTERS

The first question of this problem was:

1. Were there any differences in attitude among clusters related to achievement in those clusters?

Analysis of variance was used to answer this question. The independent variable was Cluster while the dependent variables were each of the nine attitude scales. Results of the analysis of variance are listed in Table 18 while mean ratings for each cluster on significant variables are included in Table 19.

Data in Table 18 indicate that clusters differed significantly on five attitude scales: General Attitude, Faculty, Organization, Instruction, and Instructional Analysis. The means by cluster for these five scales are listed in Table 19.

General attitude was highest in Clusters B and H, lowest in Cluster J. Faculty were rated highest in Clusters F and I, lowest in Cluster J. Organization was rated highest in Clusters H and E, lowest in Cluster J. Instructional Analysis was rated highest in Cluster F and lowest in Cluster J.

Table 18: *Analysis of Variance with Attitude as Dependent Variable and Cluster as the Independent Variable*

Variable	F Value	P
General Attitude	1.95	.04
Faculty	1.24	.27
Content	.84	.58
Organization	2.42	.01
Instruction	2.93	.002
Multicultural Study	1.54	.13
Organizational Study	.60	.80
Community Study	1.56	.12
Instructional Analysis	2.84	.003

Table 19: Means of Clusters on Five Attitude Scales

Cluster	General Attitude	Faculty	Organization	Instruction	Instructional Analysis
A	3.77	4.00	3.01	3.63	3.27
B	4.14	4.00	3.21	3.63	3.52
C	3.91	3.88	3.24	3.72	3.20
D	4.06	3.92	3.13	3.59	3.52
E	3.96	4.06	3.37	3.71	3.45
F	3.97	4.11	3.25	3.73	3.60
G	3.93	4.04	3.31	3.88	3.49
H	4.10	4.06	3.44	3.51	3.52
I	4.04	4.09	3.14	3.61	3.54
J	3.50	3.63	2.75	3.28	3.01
TOTAL	3.94	3.98	3.19	3.63	3.41

Cluster J was consistently rated lowest of all clusters on all variables. The gap between mean ratings for Cluster J and the next lowest Cluster was great, and in every case statistically significant.

Overall, the strongest ratings were given in Clusters H and F.

To determine if these attitude ratings were related to cluster achievement, the Spearman Rho correlation was computed. Attitude mean ratings were ranked by cluster, with 10 assigned to the cluster receiving the highest mean rating and one to the cluster with the lowest. This was done for each of the five attitude scales. Ranks for each cluster on total residual gains in achievement, reported in Table 11, were used in the correlation. The cluster with the highest achievement was ranked 10, the lowest one. Significant positive correlations would signal a relationship between attitude and achievement in clusters. Correlation coefficients are reported in Table 20.

Table 20: Correlations Between Total Residual Achievement and Five Attitude Scales for Clusters (n=10)

Variable	Rho
General Attitude	.18
Faculty	-.13
Organization	.36
Instruction	-.06
Instructional Analysis	.19

None of the correlations were significant, thus it was concluded that, for clusters, there was no relation between achievement and attitude.

C. ATTITUDE, PERSONAL CHARACTERISTICS, AND ACHIEVEMENT

Analysis of data for the first question was limited because of the small n due to the number of clusters in the study. It does, however, relate to the first problem which was reported in Chapter IV. The present question focuses on individual participant achievement scores, their personal characteristics, and their attitudes toward the institute. This provides potential power and precision by increasing the n from 10 to 386.

The second question related to this problem was stated as follows.

2. Was there a relation between (a) achievement and (b) attitude and personal characteristics among individual participants?

Posttest achievement on eleven sub-scale and the total test were used as one set of variables in the correlation. The nine scales and four personal characteristics were used as the second set of variables. Descriptive information on the achievement of participants is included in Table 9. Data on participant attitudes toward CMTI are presented in Table 17. Information on personal characteristics is summarized in Table 1.

The Pearson Product Moment correlation coefficient was used to determine the extent of relation except for the dichotomous variable Sex where a point biserial correlation was employed. Only those correlations that were significant at $p < .05$ are listed in Table 21.

Interpretation of data in Table 21 must be done in view of the relatively few significant correlations (27 out of 156 correlations when eight could have been anticipated by chance), and the weaknesses of the relations (none higher than .20) Three findings, however, may be drawn from these data.

1. Those persons who rated multiculture study higher tended to achieve higher on multiculture and community

Table 21: Correlation Between Achievement and Attitude and Personal Characteristics (n=386)

Variable	Community			Multiculture			Organization					
	Total	High Cog	Low Cog	Total	High Cog	Low Cog	Total	High Cog	Low Cog	High Cog	Low Cog	Total
General Attitude	.11											
Faculty	.11											
Content									-.10			
Organization									-.10			
Instruction												
Multicultural Study	.16	.11	.16	1.3		.12				.10	.13	.13
Organization Study												
Community Study												
Instructional Analyses												
Age		.13										
Sex								.14				
Instructional Level						.12	.18	.20	.10	.15	.14	.16
Teaching Experience	.12	.20					.11	.16		.19		.11

subscales. Apparently, by the end of the institute, those persons who expressed greater satisfaction with the study of other cultures and who expressed a desire to use their knowledge in working within a multicultural society also scored higher on the two subscales that tapped knowledge of such a society—the multiculture and the community subscales.

2. Instructional Level reflected a participant's preferred teaching assignment (preschool, primary, intermediate, junior high school, and senior high school). Positive correlations indicate that the higher the grade level preferred, the greater the achievement scores. Instructional Level was positively related to the study of organizations. The study of organizations was, as noted earlier, the most cognitively oriented of the content included in the institute.

3. Teaching Experience was positively related to achievement of high cognitive concepts. Those persons with greater teaching experience tended to score higher on high-cognitive concepts.

Chapter 6

CONCLUSION AND IMPLICATIONS

● *W. Robert Houston — Theodore E. Andrews*

Teaching and schooling have been known as the "domain of the young." People attended school, then they went to work. That stereotype scenario is no longer accurate. Lifelong learning is an integral and necessary phase in American culture. Business and industry are joining schools, colleges, religious institutions, and social clubs in an unbelievably complex set of learning opportunities for adults. Television, the microcomputer, and other relatively recent inventions continue to change what is considered normal living and learning conditions. Americans are growing older as a nation, with a longer life span and earlier retirement; a second or third vocation or avocation is not only desirable but necessary.

In this shifting scene, adult education is becoming more and more vital. Yet what is known about adult learning is meager. What is needed are comprehensive studies of adult motivation, adult learning styles, appropriate instructional modes for adults, and a myriad of other basic and applied research.

In the present volume, we have attempted to provide some insights that would be useful to those persons engaged in adult education, whether professionals, technicians, or citizens seeking a new skill or recreation. A comprehensive review of research on several phases of adult learning suggest a number of alternative instructional methods. Two research problems are reported here—one on the time devoted to instruction and the other on personal characteristics and attitudes, both studies using adult achievement as the dependent variable. Results of these studies are summarized in the following sections.

A. PROBLEM ONE

The purpose of Problem One was to explore, for adult learners the relation between instructional time and student achievement. Specifically, the problem as stated in null form was:

> There is no relation between time devoted to instruction of adults and their achievement, taking into consideration differences in content, level of cognition, and methods of instruction.

Achievement. To test this hypothesis, a pretest and a posttest were administered to 400 participants in a three-week Institute. These achievement tests were based on the three major conceptual topics of the Institute-community-based education, multicultural education, and organizational theory. Further, each topic was tested both in higher and lower cognitive domains.

Participant gain in achievement between pretest and posttest was significant. This was tested using both change scores (post-minus-pre scores) and residual scores. Positive and significant gains using both these measures were found for the total test and for each of its eleven subscales. Differences among clusters were fairly large, thus permitting a more valid test of the hypothesis.

Two clusters were particularly and consistently high in residual gain in achievement-clusters H and B. Three others demonstrated lower achievement than other clusters—D, A, and I.

Instructional Time. To determine the instructional time devoted to each topic and the instructional method employed, 50 twenty-minute observations were made of each cluster. Two-minute segments formed the basic unit for observation, thus 500 data units were observed for each cluster. These observations distinguished presentations, discussions, and experiential/material for each topic plus non-cognitive instruction and non-instructional periods. To determine if these fourteen dimensions were independent, thirteen mutually orthogonal contrasts were tested. Seven were significant: (1) Instruction vs. non-instruction, (2) Presentation of high cognitive vs. presentation of low cognitive concepts, (3) Total organization concepts vs. total multicultural and community concepts, (4) Total multicultural vs. total community concepts, (5) Interaction of high and low cognition with multiculture and community, (6) Presentation vs. interaction, and (7) Discussion of cognitive topics vs. experiential-cognitive topics. Differences were evident among clusters for those seven dichotomous areas of observation.

The greatest time in the workshop was used to present high cognitive multiculture topics (a mean of 19.86 percent of observations). Experiential, cognitively-related activities in community study, however, was observed only 1.48 percent of the time.

Instruction on community study averaged 13.66 percent of the time while multicultural education was studied 35.54 percent and organizational theory 33.30 percent of the time observed. Nearly half (47.62 percent) of the time was devoted to presentations, primarily at high cognitive levels (37.74 percent). Non-instructional time was less than ten percent. Clusters varied widely in the extensiveness of time each was observed engaged in the various instructional activities. These differences provided a basis for examining the relation between amount and type of instruction and participant achievement.

Time, Instruction, and Achievement. Because of its more precise measure of achievement gain, residual scores were used in examining this relation. Correlations between achievement residuals and instructional time revealed several weak but consistent relationships.

1. Presenting low cognitive material in multiculture and community was positively related to achievement of low cognitive content in those areas.

2. Presenting high cognitive material in organization was positively related to high cognitive achievement in organization.

3. Presenting low cognitive material in multiculture and community was positively related to total achievement in those areas.

4. Non-cognitive experiential activities were consistently (but not significantly) negatively related to achievement in all areas.

Based on the data presented in this monograph, it was concluded that *the relation was weak but positive between time devoted to instruction and adult achievement*. In spite of the tenuous nature of this finding, the null hypothesis of no relation was not supported. There appears to be a modest relation between time devoted to instruction of adults and their achievement, even when considering differences in content, levels of cognition, and methods of instruction.

B. PROBLEM TWO

The purpose of the second problem in the study was to explore the relation of participant attitudes and personal characteristics to adult achievement. Specifically, two questions were posed:

1. Were any differences in attitude among clusters related to achievement in those clusters?

2. Was there a relation between (a) achievement and (b) attitude and personal characteristics among individual participants?

Attitude was measured by 27 items that were related to nine scales. (1) General Attitude tapped general satisfaction with the training institute and potential use of its concepts. Specific aspects of the institute were assessed through four scales: (2) Faculty, (3) Content or substance taught in the institute, (4) Organization of the institute, and (5) Instructional strategies employed in CMTI. The last four scales related to specific content included in the institute: (6) Multiculture Study probed the impact of culture in a multicultural society, (7) Organization Study related schools to the organization of institutions, (8) Community Study focused on the community as an important element in student learning, and (9) Instructional Analysis provided introspection and analysis of instructional techniques used in the institute and those employed by teachers. The study of organizations was strongly cognitive in focus and content, while the study of communities and a multicultural society involved strong affective components.

Achievement was based on pretests and posttests of the content of institute (previously discussed as part of Problem One) while personal characteristics included variables such as age, sex, and years of teaching experience.

Faculty was the most highly rated of the nine scales, followed closely by General Attitude or general satisfaction with the institute. Organization of the institute was rated lowest.

When the four content areas were considered Multicultural Study and Community Study were rated higher than Organization Study with Instructional Analysis rated lowest. This was consistent with formal and informal comments of participants—the *instructional areas that included the strongest affective components were most highly prized.* This was evident even when conflict and tension were part of that learning process, and appeared to become stronger after a specific emotion-laden event had been completed.

Significant differences among clusters were found for five of the nine attitude scales. One cluster (J) was consistently lowest in participant ratings while two were typically high (H and F). Speculation about why this occurred did not lead to any useful hypotheses. Based on Spearman Rho correlations, *there were no significant relations between cluster mean achievement and participant attitude.*

The second question of Problem Two was posed to enable us to compare individual scores and ratings rather than group means. Increased power and precision would accrue as the *n* was increased from ten clusters to 386 individuals. The Pearson Product Moment correlation was used in these analyses except with the dichotomous variable, Sex, when the point-biserial correlation was more appropriate.

Three findings from these data were reported: (1) Those persons who rated Multicultural Study higher tended to achieve higher on multicultural and community subscales on the posttest. (2) Those persons expressing preference for higher grade levels (high school, junior high school) tended to score higher on achievement tests, particularly on the organization subscales (as noted earlier, the most cognitively-oriented of the three content areas). (3) Achievement of high cognitive concepts was positively related to years of teaching experience.

The second conclusion from the first study (process vs. task) was not tested in this study. The achievement results for the ten clusters were not significantly different. We have examined the characteristics of the five clusters that achieved the most and the five clusters that achieved the least. While the patterns support the findings of the first study, the lack of significant differences between and among these clusters makes any conclusions tentative and hypothetical.

All learning occurs in a context; for children the contextual variables are more constrained and uniformly applied. Their response mechanisms and coping skills are less well honed than those of adults. The relationship between time and achievement of children discussed in Chapter 3 appears to be stronger than those for adults. Even for children the results are not unambiguously clear. After a definitive review of the literature, Frederick and Walbert (1980) concluded: "Time devoted to school learning appears to be a modest predictor of achievement. For some types of new material, . . . time may be the best predictor. . .when material is familiar, often taught, or imprecisely measured, then time may appear weak and insignificant (193)."

Adults may be less influenced by time variables because of the varied efficiency of their individual learning styles, different motivation for understanding particular topics, increased maturation, use of a wide range of learning modes not related to time, and greater familiarity with concepts being taught. Because adult learning occurs in such a complex context, isolation of the effects of time is more difficult.

In the present study, the extent to which lower cognitive concepts were presented appeared to be interactive with time and achievement. This seemed to be particularly relevant when complex societal concepts are involved. Both community study and multicultural education provided an opportunity to test this notion, and the outcomes were consistent for both.

When a full range of concepts are considered, multivariate rather than single instructional modes may prove more effective. The traditional lecture/recitation may be appropriate for those persons who are academically able. Indeed, it is possible that our schools are biased in favor of those persons with this learning disposition.

This study raised more questions than it answered. In the study design, we were able to control certain variables such as resources, overall time, and basic instructional goals while leaving instructional strategies to individual instructional teams. Achievement was measured through direct observation. Through these controls, many of the weaknesses of previous studies were considered (e.g., using instructor *estimates* of time, Borg, 1980, 40; uncontrolled or unmatched groups, Frederick and Walberg, 1980).

What was not controlled either experimentally or statistically were learning modes of individual participants, motivations for being involved in the institute, perceptions of importance or relevance of particular topics, and perceptions of the institute.

While the number of participants was more than adequate (n=400) the research design pressed us to relate data to clusters, not individual participants, thus effectively reducing the *n* to ten. This resulted from the data set on observations to be focused on ten groups of *students*. Reanalysis of data *focusing on* individuals rather than groups could lead to more sensitive analyses.

As in almost every aspect of the study of human behavior, we have only scratched the surface. The potential may be rich, but the searchers have yet to remove the encrusted factors to see clearly the basic concepts.

References

Borg, W. R. Time and school learning. *Time to Learn*, C. Denham & A. L. Lieberman (eds.). Washington, D. C.: National Institute of Education, 1981, 33-72.

Frederick, W. C. & Walberg, H. J. Learning as a function of time, *The Journal of Educational Research* 73 (4), March/ April 1980, 183-94.

Houston, W. R., Andrews, T. C., and Bryant, B. Empirical study of institute strategies in F. T. Waterman, et al. *Designing Short-term Instructional Programs*. Washington, D. C.: Association of Teacher Educators, 1979, pp 87-146.

Chapter 7

EPILOGUE

- *Brenda L. Bryant*

"More Implications"

Dear Bob and Ted:

After our meeting last week, I was stimulated to give some thought to the study of the Corpsmember Training Institute. As you know, I was a cluster leader at CMTI. From my perspective as an Institute instructor, I have reread this study. I have examined the literature review and read most of the material cited therein. This exercise prompted my return to our recent conversation during which both of you expressed disappointment with the strength of the findings and an even greater concern that all of us profit from the study even though it probably raises more questions than it answers.

So, I begin with this question. Having examined the CMTI study, what have I learned and what intrigues me most:

I have answered this question under several headings: theoretical frame; evaluation design and methodology; subject focus; population of the study; and other variables. I have titled my responses, "More Implications."

Theoretical Frame

As I read the CMTI study, I am aware that the intent was to examine the learning of adults while using a theoretical framework that is rooted in pedagogy. The Institute's instructional design was highly prescriptive. There was a standard of uniform curriculum with system-wide objectives set by Institute leaders. As researchers, learning was defined as cognitive achievement and was presumed to occur, primarily, in-class and on-schedule.

Because the boundaries of the study were set in this manner, I believe that it became difficult to discern differences among clusters. In fact, the study was limited to factors that were given and, therefore, common among clusters and data collectors, of course, saw minimal differences.

I am suggesting that studies of adult learning be theoretically rooted in principles of adult learning. Rather than looking for the prescribed and expected outcomes, perhaps researchers can examine questions such as:

1) To what extent are students setting their own objectives and working toward achievement of those objectives?
2) To what extent are learners engaged in self evaluation?
3) To what extent are activities self-directed and self-paced?
4) To what extent are learners resources to one another?
5) To what extent is the learner able to describe how the learning will be applied in other settings?

Other questions can be raised. The point is to create a design that steers researchers toward measurement of adult achievement and toward isolation of variables that affect learning in addition to variables ordinarily examined in studies of young learners.

Evaluation Design and Methodology

In the CMTI study, researchers used a sound and scientific research design that sought quantitative and qualitative data on achievement, time-on-task, instructional approach or climate (among other things). I cannot argue with the data; in fact, they seem quite accurate from where I sit.

I am compelled, however, to propose for the future a similar study with a different kind of research design. An *action research* design would yield data on the dynamic and interactive processes that are the essence of learning. This type of design would capture changes that occur in programs and activities and learning that emerge in the instruction. This, of course, means that instead of being as unobtrusive as possible, the research would be imbedded in the program. Data would be drawn from instructors and participants on a regular basis and in an indepth and interactive process. Objective observers, who seem to capture sameness and overt behavior for the most part, would be eliminated in favor of participant researchers who, alone, can really identify uniqueness and capture elements of climate that are elusive to the distant bystander. This type of design might help us, as educators, to link the teacher, the learner, the environment and the resources in such a way as to understand better what is happening and why it is happening. Diametrically opposed to this approach is the research that is trying to isolate single or several teacher effects and link those effects to student performance. I think we are seeing that this narrow approach is not giving teachers like ourselves much to go on.

Naturally, action research is messy and poses numerous design problems. It takes a lot of time and is totally intrusive in the instructional program. But our subjects here have been teachers and future teachers. What better opportunity to understand learning than to be self-conscious about one's own learning and teaching. I happen to think that both research and practice could benefit from an action research approach to the study of adult learning.

Subject Focus

I must agree with your conclusion that the class (or the cluster, in this case) as the unit of study may not be discriminating enough to yield useful data. In the final analysis, it is individuals who learn and not groups. I would like to see us refine our understanding of the characteristics of adult learners and how these characteristics are related to learner outcomes and to teacher behaviors.

Population of the Study

The preceding remarks concerning unit of analysis raises some other questions regarding study population. The CMTI report rests on an assumption that the learner population, by virtue of age, is an adult population. I have a feeling that as we learn more about adult learning we will find that people in their twenties may not fit our requirements for adulthood. Indeed, much older persons in certain learning situations may not function as adults for a variety of reasons. We need a better definition of adult before we proceed to examine adult learning. Personal characteristics of the learner as well as environmental circumstances need to be taken into account.

My own experience with CMTI and other graduate level programs suggests to me that learners in their twenties are "transitionals" in many ways. They require elements of pedagogy and elements of andragogy in planning for their instruction. Being educated but not broadly experienced, they do not have as many intellectual hooks upon which to hang new learning as do students ten years their senior. In their early twenties, many learners need the structure, safety, consistency, order, routine, and repetition that are often part of the instruction for much younger people. Moreover, they need some ambiguity and independence and opportunities to participate in the planning and evaluation of their own learning. They need givens and objectives where the terrain is new and unvisited and they need to decide on their own objectives where the territory for study is somewhat familiar. Internal self-motivation may not be fully developed and instruction must provide some external motivators at times.

Other Variables

A number of the preceding remarks imply that we should give some attention to studying other variables related to but distinct from, the variables considered or controlled in the CMTI study. Several of these variables are listed below:

- •**Out-of-class learning**. Especially in a residential setting like CMTI, learning certainly does occur after hours. However, we know very little about the nature of this learning about the conditions which promote or impede it.

- •**Unintended outcomes**. Presumably adults set their own objectives and create many opportunities to learn, yet we have not found a way to measure those outcomes adequately.

- •**Instructor perceptions**. What the instructor intends to structure and create (in the way of direct and indirect learning experiences) does, I believe, have to be considered in attempts to characterize a learning environment. While I think these climate and design elements are observable, I am not confident that we really know what to look for when we talk about "approach to teaching" or "teaching style." The instructor himself/herself is the best source of these data.

- •**Dynamics**. Research needs to capture more of the interactive variables and not simply the static and discrete. This means taking a systems view of learning and examining the ongoing relationships between the actors and their environments.

- •**Individual learners**. We need to give more attention to individual learners and not whole classrooms as the unit for analysis of learning and achievement.

- •**Adults**. Within the adult population we ought to discriminate characteristics in addition to age that can help us understand the difference as well as the similarities among adult learners.

•**Time-on-purpose**. Adults need a purpose for learning, so the research suggests. Young adults may be less clear on purpose than older persons. Therefore, I find it important to spend quite a bit of time on creating a purpose for learning. Perhaps time-on-purpose varies directly with achievement rather than time-on the total task which may vary weakly or inversely with achievement.

I want to commend you for your idea to include an instructor in the data analysis process. This is a way, I think, to link theory and practice and to see the data in another light-something researchers often do not do.

I have enjoyed thoroughly this opportunity to reconsider the CMTI study and to reflect on my own teaching. Like you, I have raised more questions than I have answered.

Sincerely,

Brenda Bryant

APPENDICES

Appendix A   ACHIEVEMENT TEST

        Pretest and Letter of Instruction
        Scoring Key
        Posttest

Appendix B   DESCRIPTION OF CMTI CONTENT

        Organizational Theory
        Education That is Multicultural
        Community-Based Education

Appendix C   OBSERVATION INSTRUMENT

        Observer Guide
        Instructional Observation Schedule
        Directions for Checking Observation Forms

Appendix A

MEMO TO TEACHER CORPS PROJECT DIRECTORS

FROM: Floyd Waterman

RE: Pre-CMTI Data Collection

     Theodore Andrews and Robert Houston have been given the responsibility to document CMTI-79. The first part of this process is to collect pre-CMTI data. Interns and Team Leaders are to complete the enclosed questionnaires and return them prior to CMTI. Thank you for facilitating this process.

     Included in this packet are the following materials:

A. For the Project Director

     1. This Memo
     2. Director's Information Sheet

B. For the Interns and Team Leader

     Six sets of material (one for each participant and one for your files). Each set includes:

     1. Pre-CMTI Program Assessment (Directions and questions)
     2. Sample answer sheet
     3. Answer Sheet

C. Envelope addressed to the University of Nebraska, Omaha

     Would you please assist us by completing the following tasks:

     1. Set a time when your Team Leader and Interns can complete the pre-assessment. About one hour will be required.
     2. Administer the questionnaire.
     3. Complete the Director's Information Sheet.
     4. Place (a) all assessment sheets and (b) all answer sheets in return envelope.
     5. Send the envelope to the University of Nebraska, Omaha.
     6. Please mail these no later than June 9.

         This date is crucial, as is the need for returns from all (or almost all) participants by that date. If for any reason some of your Interns cannot complete this questionnaire by that time, please mail those that are completed, and have the others brought to CMTI already completed. These will be collected at registration.

If you have any questions about this, call either Bob Houston at 713/749-3621 or Ted Andrews at 703/437-3222.

DIRECTOR'S INFORMATION SHEET

Project: _____

_____

Location: _____

_____

Director's Name: _____

The Team Leader is: _____

Interns are: 1. _____

2. _____

3. _____

4. _____

Notes or Comments by Director:

PRE-CMTI PROGRAM ASSESSMENT

Prior to beginning CMTI, we are asking you to complete the following questionnaire. The purpose of this activity is to document the reactions of participants to the various experiences and outcomes of CMTI. A second questionnaire will be administered at the end of CMTI.

The data will be used to describe the group's progress and impressions. No data will be reported on individuals or on individual projects. Your responses will be kept in strictest confidence, and will not be made known to any official of Teacher Corps or Instructor in CMTI.

We have included a sample answer sheet to illustrate how the heading should be filled out and how the answers are to be recorded. Please review this sample form before filling out the answer sheet that will be returned.

Now, on the attached answer sheet, please print your name in the boxes provided for that purpose, and blacken the letter boxes as directed. Then, write the name of your project and the city where it is located. It is not necessary to complete any of the other descriptive information.

This instrument has several parts. Read the directions for each part, then blacken the appropriate space on the answer sheet. Please respond accurately and honestly to each item. Please complete all items.

When you have finished, return it with the other questionnaires from your project in the self-addressed envelope.

Thank you for your contribution.

GENERAL PURPOSE — NCS — ANSWER SHEET

SEE IMPORTANT MARKING INSTRUCTIONS ON SIDE 2

NAME (Last, First, M.I.)

Baker Tampa Florida

ANDREWS TED E

SEX

BIRTH DATE

IDENTIFICATION NUMBER

SPECIAL CODES

GRADE

BACKGROUND DATA

Please select the correct response for each item and blacken the corresponding space on the answer sheet.

1. Teacher Corps role

   A. Team Leader
   B. Intern
   C. Other

2. Age

   A. 20-24 years
   B. 25-29 years
   C. 30-34 years
   D. 35-39 years
   E. 40 years or older

3. Sex

   A. Female
   B. Male

4. Marital status

   A. Married
   B. Single

5. Number of dependent children

   A. None
   B. One
   C. Two
   D. Three
   E. Four or more

6. Race/Ethnic Group

   A. Anglo/Caucasian American
   B. Black/Afro American
   C. Asian/Pacific American
   D. Native American
   E. Hispanic/Chicano American

Background Data (continued)

7. Which of the following best describes the school your
   Teacher Corps project is located in?

   A. Rural
   B. Urban/rural
   C. Urban Inner City
   D. Other

8. At what level would you prefer to teach?

   A. Preschool, kindergarten
   B. Primary (1 - 3)
   C. Intermediate (4 - 6)
   D. Junior High (7 - 9)
   E. Senior High (10 - 12)

9. Year graduated from college

   A. 1975 - 76
   B. 1973 - 74
   C. 1971 - 72
   D. 1970 or before
   E. Not graduated

10. Major in college

    A. Social Sciences
    B. Humanities/Music/Art
    C. Science/Mathematics
    D. Industrial Arts/Technology
    E. Education and Other

11. Previous teaching experience

    A. None
    B. Student teaching only
    C. Two years or less
    D. 3 - 5 years
    E. 6 or more years

The following items are related to some of the concepts to be studied at CMTI. Read each item, then select your response. Blacken the space on the answer sheet that corresponds to your selection. In some questions, more than one choice may be correct. In such cases, be sure to select the best and most appropriate answer.

12. The president of the community action agency communicates her expectations to the school principal, the PTA president, and the Housing Authority Board. This behavior describes her:

    A. Status
    B. Role set
    C. Authority
    D. Personality reactions
    E. Priorities

13. One's tradition, life styles (e.g., behavior, values and artifacts), both contemporary and historical, reflect one's:

    A. Political party affiliation
    B. Culture
    C. Acculturation
    D. Society
    E. Education

14. As an intern or teacher which of the following should you choose to present an overview of Community Based Education to people in your school district:

    A. To Touch a Child
    B. Conrack
    C. Bridge Over the River Kwai
    D. Up the Down Staircase
    E. Star Power

15. In defining an individual's role set, you would most likely ask an employee to describe his/her:

    A. Role expectations
    B. Role relationships
    C. Role conflicts
    D. Role senders
    E. All of the above

16. Culture and ethnicity are related. On the list below the factor
    most affecting your ethnicity is:

    A. The dances you know
    B. Your place of birth
    C. The schools you have attended
    D. Your race and immigrant group
    E. Your diet

17. When each segment within the broader community to be served is
    included in the formal decision-making process, which of the follow-
    ing occurs:

    A. Leadership
    B. Accommodation
    C. Communication
    D. Representativeness
    E. All of the above

18. The degree to which members of an organization feel that they are
    being recognized for good work is a function of the dimension of
    climate called:

    A. Leadership
    B. Responsibility
    C. Power Structure
    D. Rewards
    E. Warmth

19. The "melting pot" was a conceptualization of the United States as:

    A. A culturally plural society
    B. A society in which multiethnicity was extolled
    C. A mosaic in which all could be American while retaining their
       home culture
    D. All of the above
    E. None of the above

20. The exercise of processes, authority, or procedures which move a
    group or organization toward the achievement of desired outcomes in
    a definition of:

    A. Communication
    B. Leadership
    C. Norms
    D. Life-long Learning
    E. Collaboration

21. The teacher makes a decision concerning the destination of a field
     trip following discussion with the class. This is an example of:

     A. Delegated decision
     B. Shared decision
     C. Unilateral decision
     D. A and C
     E. None of the above

22. Your class has a multiethnic population.   Which of the institutional
     problems below will give you the most concern:

     A. Discipline
     B. Language difference
     C. Administration that demands uniformity of students
     D. Time, energy, and materials to plan for individual and cultural
         differences
     E. Parents who don't understand what you are trying to accomplish

23. The process through which representatives from identified sub-communities
     are directly involved in the formal decision-making structure at all
     levels is a definition of:

     A. Communication
     B. Leadership
     C. Norms
     D. Life-long Learning
     E. Collaboration

24. Employee motivations are based on his/her own:

     A. Needs
     B. Position
     C. Group norms
     D. Coping strategy
     E. Ethnicity

25. In addition to watching for ethnic group stereotypes included in
     materials, a multicultural specialist should be aware of:

     A. The omission of minority groups except when treated as problems
         to the dominant group
     B. Distortions which either exaggerate or downplay the role of one
         group
     C. The imposition of standards which are not relevant to the group
         being discussed
     D. All of the above
     E. A and B

26. Education that is viewed as a continuing process guided by the over-riding goal of improving the quality of life for all persons, regard-less of their ages, is a definition of:

    A. Communication
    B. Leadership
    C. Norms
    D. Life-long Learning
    E. Collaboration

27. Codes of behavior based on common mores and shaped beliefs are called:

    A. Values
    B. Social structure
    C. Norms
    D. Laws
    E. Informal structures

28. People who have been assimilated into the dominant American society:

    A. Have accepted the Anglo way of life
    B. May keep their home culture
    C. May be bidialectal, bilingual, or monolingual
    D. All of the above
    E. None of the above

29. The systematic implementation of plans designed to move community attitudes from one point to another more desirable point is a definition of:

    A. Norms
    B. Change
    C. Power
    D. Culture
    E. Collaboration

30. A new teacher in a school district is told that he must march in the town's Memorial Day parade. When he protests, he is told that the teachers always march and that the school board assumes that he will be there. The expectation that all teachers will march in a town parade is an example of which of the following organizational concepts:

    A. Power
    B. Structure
    C. Authority
    D. Slippage
    E. Norms

31. A class has 70% Anglo, 20% Cuban, and 10% Black children. The curriculum should:

    A. Reflect the cultures represented in the class in the same proportion so that no group is left out and that they learn about each other's culture
    B. Help the Cuban and Black children learn to speak correctly
    C. Be conducive to intergroup understanding by presenting cross-cultural experiences
    D. Include just those elements required by the district to assume the equal education of all students in the class
    E. All of the above

32. Historically Teacher Corps interns have spent what percentage of their time working in communities:

    A. 20%
    B. 40%
    C. 50%
    D. 10%
    E. 60%

33. Which of the following is not a type of decision-making?

    A. Unilateral
    B. Shared
    C. Delegated
    D. Administrative
    E. Social

34. Those elements within a culture to which individuals and groups attach a high worth are called:

    A. Skills
    B. Values
    C. Culture
    D. Norms
    E. Slippage

35. Which of the following is an example of the change process:

    A. The school installs a loud speaker system
    B. The Community Council endorses a candidate for mayor, campaigns for her, and expects to have the Council made a permanent community agency if the candidate is elected.
    C. The Community Council raises money to build a community swimming pool
    D. The school adopts a new series of reading textbooks
    E. A and D

36. Which of the attributes below is not characteristic of an informal structure:

A. Commonality of needs
B. Indefinite duration
C. Job description
D. Variable membership
E. Commonality of concerns

37. The process of reconciling the values held in one culture with those held by a more powerful group in the society is called:

A. Sexism
B. Role Set
C. Conflict
D. Life-long Learning
E. Accommodation

38. A commitment to and provision for growth experiences for all persons in a community is a characteristic of:

A. Accommodation
B. Life-long Learning
C. Leadership
D. Collaboration
E. Power

39. Which of the following would most likely have the greatest concern that the items on this questionnaire fairly and accurately measure the content objectives of CMTI?

A. Faculty
B. Instructional Leader and Evaluators
C. Evaluators
D. Participants
E. Instructional Leader

40. The sense of belonging to a particular group of people who are linked by common geographical origin, history, language, religion, custom and tradition is called:

A. Power
B. Communication
C. Racism
D. Cultural Identity
E. Collaboration

41. If your Community Council elects its members on the basis of the sub-communities within its geographic area, it is adhering to the concept of:

   A. Accommodation
   B. Ethnicity
   C. Representativeness
   D. Collaboration
   E. Slippage

42. Schools as organizations are least likely to have:

   A. Clear, measurable goals
   B. Hierarchies
   C. Standard procedures
   D. Coercive controls
   E. Centralized decision-making

43. Any action, attitude or institutional structure which subordinates a person or group on the basis of their sex is called:

   A. Racism
   B. Accommodation
   C. Cultural Identity
   D. Conflict
   E. Sexism

44. When attempting to share information or garner support from an entire community, which of the following is the best approach:

   A. Publish articles in the local newspaper
   B. Send notices home with the school children
   C. Determine how many sub-communities exist and develop an appropriate strategy for reaching each of these
   D. Hold a Town Meeting
   E. Visit the mayor

45. Two of the attributes of the concept of slippage are:

   A. Distortion and filtering
   B. Policy and procedures
   C. Distortion and coding
   D. Coding and encoding
   E. Filtering and encoding

46. The role(s) given to women in Bridge Over the River Kwai is(are) an example of:

   A. Role Set
   B. Sexism
   C. Custom
   D. Collaboration
   E. Racism

47. When designing a life-long learning program in your community, which of the following activities is not appropriate:

   A. A "new games" program at the local nursing home
   B. A portable library which makes home visits
   C. A career education center open to persons of all ages
   D. An adult education program based on a community-wide needs assessment
   E. None of the above

48. French and Raven define five typologies of power. Which of the five listed below is not one of the five typologies?

   A. Normative
   B. Reward
   C. Coercive
   D. Expert
   E. Legitimate

49. Continuing efforts to desegregate our schools and society illustrate the concept of:

   A. Life-long Learning
   B. Collaboration
   C. Communication
   D. Powerlessness
   E. Accommodation

50. A Training Complex designed to respond to the training needs of all teachers, aides, administrators, and other school staff has met only a limited set of educational needs because:

   A. Multicultural education has not been identified as a major training need
   B. School-based programs are too narrow in their focus
   C. The training needs of the entire community have not been considered
   D. Such programs cannot meet the needs of so many different parties
   E. Administrators should not be included

51. The students generally agree that they are taking Course 123 to
    learn to teach Johnny to read. The instructor chooses to teach
    theories of reading. The conflict that results is based upon dis-
    cordance between:

    A. Means
    B. Goals
    C. Resources
    D. Message channels
    E. Informal groups

52. The lack of the capacity to have an impact on or to be able to
    influence the course of events in an organization or on personal or
    group behavior is a definition of:

    A. Slippage
    B. Leadership
    C. Conflict
    D. Powerlessness
    E. Motivation

53. The group or individual within the Teacher Corps Community that has
    the ultimate responsibility for leadership in the Project is:

    A. The Director
    B. The Community Council
    C. The Policy Board
    D. The Institution of Higher Education
    E. The Local Education Agency

54. In the film, Bridge on the River Kwai, power is ultimately a function of:

    A. Authority
    B. Expertise
    C. Rank
    D. Regulations
    E. Friendship

55. During his first days of teaching at Calvin Coolidge High School,
    Sylvia Barrett encountered feelings of:

    A. Elation
    B. Powerlessness
    C. Comfort
    D. Depression
    E. Joy

56. Which of the following would most likely succeed in breaking up a
    neighborhood:

    A. The election of a new mayor
    B. Receiving an urban redevelopment grant for the inner city
    C. Building a new expressway around the city
    D. Building a new airport 30 miles from downtown
    E. All of the above

57. Conflict can occur when there is discordance over:

    A. Goals
    B. Values
    C. Means
    D. Status
    E. All of the above

58. An element in accommodation is:

    A. Conflict
    B. Racism
    C. Slippage
    D. Collaboration
    E. Powerlessness

59. Which of the following words best represents the essence of a
    Teacher Corps Project:

    A. Accommodation
    B. Collaboration
    C. Leadership
    D. Community
    E. Communication

60. The process of which information is transmitted or exchanged through
    symbols, signs, or behaviors is called:

    A. Collaboration
    B. Representativeness
    C. Communication
    D. Slippage
    E. Accommodation

61. Any attitude, action or institutional structure which subordinates
    a person or group because of color is called:

    A. Sexism
    B. Cultural Identity
    C. Accommodation
    D. Racism
    E. Role Set

62. "Noah made a list of ways school people might be more considerate of
    the Ways of the People in their teaching practices. He talked his
    idea over with the Team Leader, who was also an Anglo, and she
    encouraged Noah to work with the Community Coordinator. She cautioned
    Noah though, and told him that the school's regular teachers had their
    own ways of doing things."

    The above paragraph indicated that Noah is sensitive to the problems of:

    A. Change
    B. Collaboration
    C. Racism
    D. Accommodation
    E. Leadership

63. When disagreements occur between faculty members in a school, it is
    a good idea to consider first if the problem is one of:

    A. Slippage
    B. Role set
    C. Temporary systems
    D. Communication
    E. Motivation

64. Which of the below is(are) learned and inculcated by the sanction
    established by the group:

    A. Norms
    B. Accommodation
    C. Collaboration
    D. Sexism
    E. Values

65. Persons will have trouble dealing with questions concerning value
    systems and loyalty if they accept the following change theory:

    A. Economic Strategy
    B. Academic Strategy
    C. Fellowship Strategy
    D. Military Strategy
    E. Political Strategy

66. Which of the following change strategies was <u>not</u> included in Kurt E. Olmsok's, "Seven Pure Strategies of Change":

    A. Personal Strategy
    B. Political Strategy
    C. Economic Strategy
    D. Military Strategy
    E. Fellowship Strategy

67. The problems that occurred in Buena Vista were primarily the result of conflict over:

    A. Cultural values
    B. Norms
    C. Leadership
    D. Collaboration
    E. Power

68. The hypothesis that shared power will result in more effective programs of pre and inservice and community education relies on a belief in:

    A. Accommodation
    B. Motivation
    C. Communication
    D. Community
    E. Collaboration

69. Schools as bureaucratic organizations are not likely to:

    A. Have centralized decision-making procedures
    B. Have standardized salary scales
    C. Approve textbooks
    D. Change easily
    E. All of the above

70. America's capitalistic society has contributed to which of the following feelings often expressed by the country's minority populations?

    A. Happiness
    B. Powerlessness
    C. Success
    D. Power
    E. Frustration

71. The essential quality that an effective administrator must possess is:

A. Sense of humor
B. Leadership
C. Concern for fairness
D. A humanistic viewpoint
E. A rigid moral code

KEY TO PRE-TEST

12.	B	Role Set - High		49.	E	Accomm. - High
13.	D	Culture - Low		50.	C	LLL - High
14.	A	Comm. - High		51.	B	Conflict - High
15.	E	Role Set - Low		52.	D	Powerless - Low
16.	D	Culture - High		53.	C	Lead. - High
17.	D	Repre. - Low		54.	B	Power - High
18.	D	Formal - High		55.	B	Powerless - High
19.	E	Cult. Iden. - High		56.	B	Comm. - High
20.	B	Leadership - Low		57.	E	Conflict - Low
21.	B	Dec. Making - High		58.	A	Accomm. - Low
22.	D	Culture - High		59.	B	Coll. - High
23.	E	Coll. - Low		60.	C	Comm. - Low
24.	A	Motiv. - Low		61.	D	Racism - Low
25.	D	Values - High		62.	A	Change - High
26.	D	L-L-L - Low		63.	D	Comm. High
27.	C	Norms - Low		64.	E	Values - Low
28.	A	Racism - Low		65.	E	Change - Low
29.	B	Change - Low		66.	A	Change - Low
30.	E	Norms - High		67.	A	Values - High
31.	A	Racism - High		68.	E	Coll. - Low
32.	B	Comm. - Low		69.	D	Change - High
33.	E	Dec. Making - Low		70.	B	Powerless - High
34.	B	Values - Low		71.	E	Lead. - High
35.	B	Change - High				
36.	C	Formal - Low				
37.	E	Accomm. - Low				
38.	B	LLL - Low				
39.	B	Motivat - High				
40.	D	Cul. Iden - Low				
41.	C	Represt. - Low				
42.	A	Slippage - High				
43.	E	Sexism - Low				
44.	C	Repres. - High				
45.	A	Slippage - Low				
46.	B	Sexism - High				
47.	E	LLL - High				
48.	A	Power - Low				

POSTTEST

The following items are related to some of the concepts studied at CMTI. Read each item, then select your response. Blacken the space on the answer sheet that corresponds to your selection. In some questions, more than one choice may be correct. In such cases, be sure to select the best and most appropriate answer.

1. If your Community Council elects its members on the basis of the sub-communities within its geographic area, it is adhering to the concept of:

   A. Accommodation
   B. Ethnicity
   C. Representativeness
   D. Collaboration
   E. Slippage

2. The sense of belonging to a particular group of people who are linked by common geographical origin, history, language, religion, custom and tradition is called:

   A. Power
   B. Communication
   C. Racism
   D. Cultural Identity
   E. Collaboration

3. Which of the following would most likely have the greatest concern that the items on this questionnaire fairly and accurately measure the content objectives of CMTI?

   A. Faculty
   B. Instructional Leader and Evaluators
   C. Evaluators
   D. Participants
   E. Instructional Leader

4. A commitment to and provision for growth experiences for all persons in a community is a characteristic of:

   A. Accommodation
   B. Life-long Learning
   C. Leadership
   D. Collaboration
   E. Power

5. The process of reconciling the values held in one culture with those
   held by a more powerful group in the society is called:

   A. Sexism
   B. Role Set
   C. Conflict
   D. Life-long Learning
   E. Accommodation

6. Which of the attributes below is not characteristic of an informal
   structure:

   A. Commonality of needs
   B. Indefinite duration
   C. Job description
   D. Variable membership
   E. Commonality of concerns

7. Which of the following is an example of the change process:

   A. The school installs a loud speaker system
   B. The Community Council endorses a candidate for mayor, campaigns
      for her, and expects to have the Council made a permanent com-
      munity agency if the candidate is elected.
   C. The Community Council raises money to build a community swimming
      pool.
   D. The school adopts a new series of reading textbooks
   E. A and D

8. Those elements within a culture to which individuals and groups
   attach a high worth are called:

   A. Skills
   B. Values
   C. Culture
   D. Norms
   E. Slippage

9. Which of the following is not a type of decision-making?

   A. Unilateral
   B. Shared
   C. Delegated
   D. Administrative
   E. Social

10. Historically Teacher Corps interns have spent what percentage of their time working in communities:

    A. 20%
    B. 40%
    C. 50%
    D. 10%
    E. 60%

11. A class has 70% Anglo, 20% Cuban, and 10% Black children. The curriculum should:

    A. Reflect the cultures represented in the class in the same proportion so that no group is left out and that they learn about each other's culture
    B. Help the Cuban and Black children learn to speak correctly
    C. Be conducive to intergroup understanding by presenting cross-cultural experiences
    D. Include just those elements required by the district to assume the equal education of all students in the class
    E. All of the above

12. A new teacher in a school district is told that he must march in the town's Memorial Day parade. When he protests, he is told that the teachers always march and that the school board assumes that he will be there. The expectation that all teachers will march in a town parade is an example of which of the following organizational concepts:

    A. Power
    B. Structure
    C. Authority
    D. Slippage
    E. Norms

13. The systematic implementation of plans designed to move community attitudes from one point to another more desirable point is a definition of:

    A. Norms
    B. Change
    C. Power
    D. Culture
    E. Collaboration

14. People who have been assimilated into the dominant American society:

    A. Have accepted the Anglo way of life
    B. May keep their home culture
    C. May be bidialectal, bilingual, or monolingual
    D. All of the above
    E. None of the above

15. Codes of behavior based on common mores and shaped beliefs are called:

    A. Values
    B. Social structure
    C. Norms
    D. Laws
    E. Informal structures

16. Education that is viewed as a continuing process guided by the over-
    riding goal of improving the quality of life for all persons, regard-
    less of their ages, is a definition of:

    A. Communication
    B. Leadership
    C. Norms
    D. Life-long Learning
    E. Collaboration

17. In addition to watching for ethnic group stereotypes included in
    materials, a multicultural specialist should be aware of:

    A. The omission of minority groups except when treated as problems
       to the dominant group
    B. Distortions which either exaggerate or downplay the role of one
       group
    C. The imposition of standards which are not relevant to the group
       being discussed
    D. All of the above
    E. A and B

18. Employee motivations are based on his/her own:

    A. Needs
    B. Position
    C. Group norms
    D. Coping strategy
    E. Ethnicity

19. The process through which representatives from identified sub-communities
    are directly involved in the formal decision-making structure at all
    levels is a definition of:

    A. Communication
    B. Leadership
    C. Norms
    D. Life-long Learning
    E. Collaboration

20. Your class has a multiethnic population. Which of the institutional problems below will give you the most concern:

   A. Discipline
   B. Language difference
   C. Administration that demands uniformity of students
   D. Time, energy, and materials to plan for individual and cultural differences
   E. Parents who don't understand what you are trying to accomplish

21. The teacher makes a decision concerning the destination of a field trip following discussion with the class. This is an example of:

   A. Delegated decision
   B. Shared decision
   C. Unilateral decision
   D. A and C
   E. None of the above

22. The exercise of processes, authority, or procedures which move a group or organization toward the achievement of desired outcomes in a definition of:

   A. Communication
   B. Leadership
   C. Norms
   D. Life-long Learning
   E. Collaboration

23. In upstate New York, native Americans who live on reservations often commute daily to factories where they have full time jobs. This life style is an illustration of:

   A. Collaboration
   B. Life-long learning
   C. Communication
   D. Formal Structure
   E. Accommodation

24. The degree to which members of an organization feel that they are being recognized for good work is a function of the dimension of climate called:

   A. Leadership
   B. Responsibility
   C. Power Structure
   D. Rewards
   E. Warmth

25. When each segment within the broader community to be served is
    included in the formal decision-making process, which of the follow-
    ing occurs:

    A. Leadership
    B. Accommodation
    C. Communication
    D. Representativeness
    E. All of the above

26. Culture and ethnicity are related. On the list below the factor
    most affecting your ethnicity is:

    A. The dances you know
    B. Your place of birth
    C. The schools you have attended
    D. Your race and immigrant group
    E. Your diet

27. In defining an individual's role set, you would most likely ask an
    employee to describe his/her:

    A. Role expectations
    B. Role relationships
    C. Role conflicts
    D. Role senders
    E. All of the above

28. As an intern or teacher which of the following should you choose to
    present an overview of Community Based Education to people in your
    school district:

    A. To Touch a Child
    B. Conrack
    C. Bridge Over the River Kwai
    D. Up the Down Staircase
    E. Star Power

29. One's tradition, life styles (e.g., behavior, values and artifacts),
    both contemporary and historical, reflect one's:

    A. Political party affiliation
    B. Culture
    C. Acculturation
    D. Society
    E. Education

30. The president of the community action agency communicates her expectations to the school principal, the PTA president, and the Housing Authority Board. This behavior describes her:

    A. Status
    B. Role set
    C. Authority
    D. Personality reactions
    E. Priorities

31. The essential quality that an effective administrator must possess is:

    A. Sense of humor
    B. Leadership
    C. Concern for fairness
    D. A humanistic viewpoint
    E. A rigid moral code

32. America's capitalistic society has contributed to which of the following feelings often expressed by the country's minority populations?

    A. Happiness
    B. Powerlessness
    C. Success
    D. Power
    E. Frustration

33. Schools as bureaucratic organizations are not likely to:

    A. Have centralized decision-making procedures
    B. Have standardized salary scales
    C. Approve textbooks
    D. Change easily
    E. All of the above

34. The hypothesis that shared power will result in more effective programs of pre and inservice and community education relies on a belief in:

    A. Accommodation
    B. Motivation
    C. Communication
    D. Community
    E. Collaboration

35. The problems that occurred in Buena Vista were primarily the result of conflict over:

    A. Cultural values
    B. Norms
    C. Leadership
    D. Collaboration
    E. Power

36. Which of the following change strategies was not included in Kurt E. Olmsok's "Seven Pure Strategies of Change":

    A. Personal Strategy
    B. Political Strategy
    C. Economic Strategy
    D. Military Strategy
    E. Fellowship Strategy

37. Persons will have trouble dealing with questions concerning value systems and loyalty if they accept the following change theory:

    A. Economic Strategy
    B. Academic Strategy
    C. Fellowship Strategy
    D. Military Strategy
    E. Political Strategy

38. Which of the below is(are) learned and inculcated by the sanction established by the group:

    A. Norms
    B. Accommodation
    C. Collaboration
    D. Sexism
    E. Values

39. When disagreements occur between faculty members in a school, it is a good idea to consider first if the problem is one of:

    A. Slippage
    B. Role set
    C. Temporary systems
    D. Communication
    E. Motivation

40. "Noah made a list of ways school people might be more considerate of the Ways of the People in their teaching practices. He talked his idea over with the Team Leader, who was also an Anglo, and she encouraged Noah to work with the Community Coordinator. She cautioned Noah though, and told him that the school's regular teachers had their own ways of doing things."

The above paragraph indicates that Noah needs to be more sensitive to problems related to:

A. Change
B. Collaboration
C. Racism
D. Accommodation
E. Leadership

41. Any attitude, action or institutional structure which subordinates a person or group because of color is called:

A. Sexism
B. Cultural Identity
C. Accommodation
D. Racism
E. Role Set

42. The process of which information is transmitted or exchanged through symbols, signs, or behaviors is called.

A. Collaboration
B. Representativeness
C. Communication
D. Slippage
E. Accommodation

43. Which of the following words best represents the essence of a Teacher Corps Project:

A. Accommodation
B. Collaboration
C. Leadership
D. Community
E. Communication

44. An element in accommodation is:

A. Conflict
B. Racism
C. Slippage
D. Collaboration
E. Powerlessness

45. Conflict can occur when there is discordance over:

    A. Goals
    B. Values
    C. Means
    D. Status
    E. All of the above

46. Which of the following would most likely succeed in breaking up a neighborhood:

    A. The election of a new mayor
    B. Receiving an urban redevelopment grant for the inner city
    C. Building a new expressway around the city
    D. Building a new airport 30 miles from downtown
    E. All of the above

47. During his first days of teaching at Calvin Coolidge High School, Sylvia Barrett encountered feelings of:

    A. Elation
    B. Powerlessness
    C. Comfort
    D. Depression
    E. Joy

48. In the film, Bridge on the River Kwai, power is ultimately a function of:

    A. Authority
    B. Expertise
    C. Rank
    D. Regulations
    E. Friendship

49. The group or individual within the Teacher Corps Community that has the ultimate responsibility for leadership in the Project is:

    A. The Director
    B. The Community Council
    C. The Policy Board
    D. The Institution of Higher Education
    E. The Local Education Agency

50. The lack of the capacity to have an impact on or to be able to influence the course of events in an organization or on personal or group behavior is a definition of:

    A. Slippage
    B. Leadership
    C. Conflict
    D. Powerlessness
    E. Motivation

51. The students generally agree that they are taking Course 123 to learn to teach Johnny to read. The instructor chooses to teach theories of reading. The conflict that results is based upon discordance between:

    A. Means
    B. Goals
    C. Resources
    D. Message channels
    E. Informal groups

52. A Training Complex which responds only to the training needs of teachers, aides, administrators, and other school staff has met a limited set of educational needs because:

    A. Multicultural education has not been identified as a major training need
    B. School-based programs are too narrow in their focus
    C. The training needs of the entire community have not been considered
    D. Such programs cannot meet the needs of so many different parties
    E. Administrators should not be included

53. Juanita's mother has organized parents to prevent their Hispanic children from eating lunch at school where the food is different from what the children eat at home. Juanita's mother's conduct may be illustrative of her desire to retain her:

    A. Racism
    B. Cultural Identity
    C. Role Set
    D. Sexism
    E. Hierarchy

54. French and Raven define five typologies of power. Which of the five listed below is not one of the five typologies?

    A. Normative
    B. Reward
    C. Coercive
    D. Expert
    E. Legitimate

55. When designing a life-long learning program in your community, which
    of the following activities is <u>not</u> appropriate:

    A. A "new games" program at the local nursing home
    B. A portable library which makes home visits
    C. A career education center open to persons of all ages
    D. An adult education program based on a community-wide needs
        assessment
    E. None of the above

56. The role(s) given to women in <u>Bridge Over the River Kwai</u> is(are)
    an example of:

    A. Role Set
    B. Sexism
    C. Custom
    D. Collaboration
    E. Racism

57. Two of the attributes of the concept of slippage are:

    A. Distortion and filtering
    B. Policy and procedures
    C. Distortion and coding
    D. Coding and encoding
    E. Filtering and encoding

58. When attempting to share information or garner support from an entire
    community, which of the following is the best approach:

    A. Publish articles in the local newspaper
    B. Send notices home with the school children
    C. Determine how many sub-communities exist and develop an
        appropriate strategy for reaching each of these
    D. Hold a Town Meeting
    E. Visit the mayor

59. Any action, attitude or institutional structure which subordinates
    a person or group on the basis of their sex is called:

    A. Racism
    B. Accommodation
    C. Cultural Identity
    D. Conflict
    E. Sexism

60. Schools as organizations are least likely to have:

    A. Clear, measurable goals
    B. Hierarchies
    C. Standard procedures
    D. Coercive controls
    E. Centralized decision-making

FEELINGS ABOUT CMTI

Please read the statements below and mark the position on the attached **answer** sheet which best expresses your feelings or opinions about CMTI.

A. Strongly Disagree

B. Disagree

C. Neutral

D. Agree

E. Strongly Agree

61. Generally, CMTI was a very good experience.

62. The faculty encouraged the development of new viewpoints and appreciations.

63. The content included in CMTI was not adequate.

64. The way CMTI was organized resulted in better participant learning.

65. Textbooks, simulations, readings, and other materials were poor and inadequate.

66. The multicultural environment at CMTI enriched me personally.

67. CMTI increased my knowledge and skills in studying organizations.

68. I plan to do some things next year differently because of a greater understanding and appreciation of the community.

69. Because of the instructional analyses sessions, I will teach differently.

70. I would recommend CMTI to others.

71. The faculty had a thorough knowledge of the subject matter being taught.

72. Many of the ideas, concepts, and content included in CMTI were new to me.

73. I was often confused by the procedures and processes used.

74. Activities were interesting and well designed.

75. CMTI increased my knowledge of other cultures.

76. I now have a new appreciation of the importance of studying organizations.

77. Understanding school communities is more important than I used to think it was.

78. I appreciate the importance of planning for and analyzing instruction.

79. I plan to use CMTI knowledge and skills in my professional career.

80. The faculty seemed to be interested in participants as persons.

81. CMTI increased my general knowledge and skills.

82. More educational experiences should be organized this way.

83. I learn more when other methods of instruction are used.

84. Because of multicultural experiences at CMTI, I am likely to change my professional actions in the future.

85. Because of what I learned about organizations, I will make decisions and act differently in the future.

86. CMTI increased my knowledge of and skills in, working with a school community.

87. I understand more about the instructional process.

TRAINING MATERIALS

We would appreciate your reaction to some of the materials that were available during CMTI. Using the five point scale below, please mark on the answer sheet your personal feeling about each of the items.

          A. Do Not Remember Using

          B. Not Helpful

          C. Of Some Help

          D. Helpful

          E. Very Helpful

88. Perspectives on Organizations
Volume I - The School as a Social Organization   Corwin & Edelfelt

89. Perspectives on Organizations
Volume II - Schools in the Larger Social Order   Corwin & Edelfelt

90. Perspectives on Organizations
Volume III - Viewpoints for Teachers   Corwin & Edelfelt

91. Teacher Corps Portraits
Four Case Studies   Savage

92. In Praise of Diversity: A Resource Book
for Multicultural Education   Gold, Grant & Rivlin

93. In Praise of Diversity: Classroom Application   Grant

94. Multicultural Education: A Functional
Bibliography for Teachers   Gold, Grant & Rivlin

95. The Schooling of Native America   Thompson

96. Community Involvement for Classroom Teachers   Hager

97. Temporary Systems   Gant, South & Hansen

OPEN ENDED QUESTION

If you would like to make any statement about CMTI, please do so in the following space. In no case will a comment be reported from a specific individual; however; the general nature of any and all comments will be reported.

Appendix B

DESCRIPTION OF CMTI CONTENT

CONTENT AREA 1: ORGANIZATIONAL THEORY

Rationale

The Teacher Corps is a teacher training program. Corpsmemembers--
Interns and Team Leaders--work in schools and communities. Their
preparation seeks to help them become the best teachers possible. As
one of their initial Teacher Corps experiences, the CMTI is intended,
in part, to help Corpsmembers enter and function appropriately in their
local settings. In short, the CMTI is intended to help Corpsmembers
prepare to undertake their training for the education professions. What,
then, does the study of organizations have to do with those purposes?

First, a quick look at history. The Teacher Corps grew from the
activism, social concern, and "change posture" of the mid-1960s. Early
projects often had as many as 35 Interns each. Those facts often combined
to create problems in local schools and communities when Interns and
(to a much lesser extent, Team Leaders) perceived themselves as change
agents, individuals who knew best what should be "fixed" in the schools
and communities where they were working.

The Teacher Corps learned a great deal from the problems which early
projects had in dealing with the existing permanent systems with whom--
and within which--they were working. Research by Corwin and others
suggested that the study of organizational theory and dynamics would help
Corpsmembers to better understand the school and community structures with
which they worked. They pointed out that the school is, after all, an
organization. And communities are made up of a myriad of organizations.

Such organizations, we have too often assumed, do not themselves behave according to certain patterns which are discernible and can be described. We have assumed that only people behave. But organizations do behave. If organizational behavior can be understood by the individuals in an organization, it can be dealt with and even used to enhance the functioning of the organization as it responds to internal and external stimuli. If Corpsmembers become more familiar with the phenomena of organizational behavior, they will come to understand the schools and communities in which they work. Such understanding is prerequisite to effective teaching. Tanner and others have identified certain crucial organizational concepts for study at the CMTI. The selected concepts are those seen as most appropriate to CMTI and Teacher Corps goals.

Finally, the classroom is also an organization. As they move from observation in the classroom to small-group tutoring and finally to teaching, Interns can be expected to draw upon organizational theory to help them understand classroom dynamics. Their teaching will be more effective if they recognize, understand, and apply organizational concepts and dynamics in the classroom. In short, the study of organizations of and organizational concepts will help to prepare Corpsmembers for appropriate entry and functioning in the classroom, school, and community organizations of which they will be a part.

The Basic Organizational Concepts and Their Definitions

INFLUENCE is the capacity to have an impact on the course of events in an organization or on the behavior of a group or a person.

POWER is the capacity to require specified behavior.

AUTHORITY is the right to direct the behavior of others, and to do
so on the basis of position.

MOTIVATION is readiness to behave in ways which individuals perceive
as likely to satisfy their own needs.

COMMUNICATION is the process by which information is shared.

CONFLICT is the presence of discordance within, between, or among
individuals, groups, and/or organizations.

DECISION-MAKING is the process of making judgements and choices.

NORMS are standards that govern the behavior of individuals in
particular settings.

ROLE SET is a constellation of relationships which an individual
has by virtue of occupying a particular position in an
organization.

ORGANIZATIONAL STRUCTURE is the pattern of relationships among
roles or positions in an organization.

FORMAL STRUCTURE is the planned pattern of relationships based upon
the mission and technical requirements of the organization.

INFORMAL STRUCTURE is the emergent patterns of relationships that are
not called for by the mission or technical requirements of
the organization.

SLIPPAGE is that distortion which occurs as policy and/or information
are transmitted within the organizational structure.

Organizational Theory Objectives

1. Participants will understand and be able to identify and describe

the basic components which define organizations, both as they exist independently and as they interact with one another.

2. Participants will understand and be able to apply selected organizational concepts in school and community settings.

3. Participants will understand and be able to describe their probable roles as Interns and Team Leaders and the organizational factors which influence those roles in several Teacher Corps contexts (i.e., the project, the local school, community, and the national program).

4. Participants will develop and implement a plan to study the CMTI as an organization.

5. Participants will develop a preliminary plan for collecting and analyzing organizational data in their local project setting.

CONTENT AREA 2: EDUCATION THAT IS MULTICULTURAL

Rationale

The reality of our culturally pluralistic society is now being acknowledged. With this has come the recognition that we must move beyond the monocultural perspectives that have traditionally influenced our educational processes and interpersonal behavior. If students are to be prepared to function effectively in a culturally pluralistic society, they must be provided with new types of skills, knowledge, and attitudes. They must acquire the skill of functioning effectively, both in their own and in other ethnic communities. They must also accept the right of different ethnic groups to exist and develop positive attitudes about the life styles and value systems of the various cultural groups which comprise our diverse society. Finally, they must acquire accurate knowledge of the history and cultural heritage of a number of cultural groups. Multicultural education, thus perceived, will result in an improvement in the quality of education offered to all children. It will also assist in the creation of those attitudes which will aid in the elimination of discriminatory practices based on race, sex, class, age, and physical handicaps.

This focus on education for life in a culturally diverse society has important implications for the preparation of teachers. Most preservice teachers have been educated in a system that has been, up to now, largely monocultural. It is therefore of crucial importance that teachers be helped to acquire the knowledge, skills, and attitudes which are important for effective functioning in a culturally diverse society and

which they are expected to transmit to students. Teachers also
need to understand how curriculum, instructional strategies, administrative practices, classroom environment, and school-community
relations affect a program of education that is multicultural. It is
also important that they develop skill in recognizing the factors in
the everyday quality of classroom living that stimulate or inhibit the
development of multicultural learning environments.

The experience of working through the concepts as they apply to
education that is multicultural, and of engaging in the various activities
in the content strand (plus the actual experience of multicultural living
at CMTI) will assist in the acquisition of such skills, knowledge,
attitudes, and changed behaviors.

Multicultural Education: A Working Definition

Multicultural Education has as its goal the development of individuals
who will be able to function effectively in a culturally diverse society.
This mandates the type of structured educational processes that will:

1) Develop self acceptance and pride in one's own culture.

2) Develop acceptance, understanding, and appreciation of other
   cultures and respect for those cultures.

3) Provide accurate knowledge about the life, history, heritage,
   lifestyles, and value systems of other cultures.

4) Develop appreciation of cultural diversity and the way in which
   it contributes to the strength of the nation.

The Basic Multicultural Concepts and Their Definitions

CULTURE is represented by the behavior patterns, values, beliefs, symbols,

and institutions developed by members of a society
which distinguish those members from members of other
groups.

CULTURAL IDENTITY is the sense of belonging to a particular group of
people who are linked by common geographical origin,
history, language, religion, custom, and tradition.

POWERLESSNESS is the lack of capacity to have an impact on or to
influence the course of events in an organization or on
personal or group behavior.

VALUES are those elements within a culture to which individuals and
groups attach a high worth.

RACISM is represented by practices and actions by individuals or
institutions based on the belief that one race is
inherently superior to others and has the right to
dominate those races considered to be inferior.

SEXISM is represented by practices and actions based on the belief that
one sex is inherently superior to another and has the right
to dominate the sex considered to be inferior.

ACCOMMODATION is the process of reconciling the values held in one's
culture with those held by a more powerful group within
the society.

Multicultural Education Objectives

    To demonstrate their knowledge of concepts relevant to the educational
needs of children in a pluralistic society, participants will acquire certain
skills in the pursuit of the following objectives:

Cognitive Objectives

1. Define and provide a rationale for education that is multicultural.

2. Define the concepts listed below and give examples of the way that these can influence the development of education that is multicultural:

    a) communication

    b) culture

    c) cultural identity

    d) conflict

    e) power/powerlessness

    f) values

    g) racism

    h) sexism

    i) accomodation

3. Identify the ways in which race, culture, ethnicity, and class impact can influence one's own personality and lifestyle and those of others.

4. Distinguish myths and stereotypes from factual information about individual and cultural diversity.

5. Recognize that biases exist in school materials and public media.

6. Recognize unacceptable behavior resulting from prejudice and discrimination based on race, ethnicity, culture, sex, age, class, physical characteristics, and religion.

7. Acquire basic information concerning the life, history, culture, values, and lifestyle of selected cultural groups.

8. Identify the causes of prejudice, discrimination, racism, and sexism and the manner in which American institutions perpetuate those phenomena.

Affective Objectives

9. Demonstrate growth in understanding of the norms, values, beliefs,

and attitudes which people hold as they relate to cultural and individual diversity.

10. Exhibit behavior and attitudes which reflect respect for and acceptance of the value, dignity, and worth of individuals and groups different from themselves.

11. Work effectively with others of both sexes and of diverse racial, ethnic, cultural, age, and religious groups in performing the tasks of the CMTI experience.

Analysis Objectives

12. Analyze both instructional materials and the media for race and sex bias.

Practice in Synthesis Objectives

In role playing, simulation exercises, and hands-on experiences, participants will:

13. Demonstrate skill in observation and analysis by identifying those factors listed below which inhibit or stimulate the development of education that is multicultural:

   a) Staffing patterns

   b) Curricula

   c) Acceptance or rejection of linguistic and language differences

   d) Choice of instructional materials

   e) School-community relations

CONTENT AREA 3:   COMMUNITY-BASED EDUCATION

Rationale

Technological change in our society has far outrun our ability to
adapt and adjust to a new way of life. Many Americans are frustrated and
alienated, and too many feel powerless to change even the simplest of
things which directly affect their lives. We live in the context of
bigness, loss of control, and mistrust. In that context, governmental,
educational, business, and community leaders at all levels are struggling
to find more effective, efficient ways of preparing both the young and
the old to cope with ever-changing problems of delivering human services
and of designing human development systems to better meet community and
individual needs. In this country, the question is not so much where to
find the resources to solve the complex problems which face us, but how
to effectively develop the local leadership to organize and coordinate
the multi-resources available.

The dilemma in which our society and our schools find themselves
paradoxically holds great potential for educational institutions to perform
their basic missions better than ever. Program modification and a building
of trust among communities, schools, and colleges are required. Such
collaborative relationships, both in spirit and through formal agreements,
aimed at joint, mutually beneficial efforts to solve pressing social
problems and to improve the quality of life of all citizens seem mandated
by public reaction and economic necessity. Community-based education is
one attempt to provide the needed leadership and to encourage such
collaboration.

The Teacher Corps's traditional involvement with community affairs
has distinguished it from many other federal programs. In fact,
community involvement lies at the very heart of its success:

> As with any other thrust, Teacher Corps community involvememt
> and its manner of implementation varies from project to project.
> However, common to all programs is the desire to meet particular
> community needs.[1]

While the Teacher Corps has distinguished itself in the area of
community education and involvement, many Teacher Corps watchers also
point to this area as generally being the weakest component in local
projects. Results of a study of ten Teacher Corps projects in operation
during 1969-1970 show that:

> . . . fewer than a third of the university people, and only half
> as many school people, considered the community activity component
> excellent. More than a quarter of the interns said it was unsatis-
> factory or non-existent; most thought it less valuable than the
> teaching experience. Between a quarter and a third of university
> and school people said that if any part of the program was reduced,
> it should be the community work.[2]

More recently, William L. Smith, the Director of the Teacher Corps
program, stated that community-based education has emerged as one of the
most vital components of the Teacher Corps:

> Teacher Corps projects mobilized community resources and leadership
> for community-based education. Historically, interns have spent
> about 20 per cent of their internship in school-community activities.
> The variety of community education activities is legion, ranging
> from home tutoring programs to the development of bilingual, multi-
> cultural education programs for community residents. Through
> Teacher Corps, community volunteers have become an integral part of
> the school experiences of their children. Teacher Corps projects
> now have school-community councils which are an essential part of
> the life of a project.[3]

---

1   p. 13, "Ten Years of Teacher Corps, 1966-1967" published by Teacher
    Corps under Contract USOE No. 300-75-0103.
2   pp. 33-34, "Lessons from the Teacher Corps," 1974, a publication of
    the National Education Association.
3. op. cit. "Ten Years of Teacher Corps," p. 2.

It is obvious that the Teacher Corps has a historical and
philosophical commitment to education that is emerging as a fully
developed conceptual and operational model based on both the process
of community involvement in assessment and decision-making, and the
delivery of needed services and programs to the school and community.
Interns and Team Leaders are vital to this commitment, and to the
continued evolution of a functioning, efficient community-based
education model. Thus, the CMTI offers its participants curriculum
in community-based education which will help Interns and Team Leaders
to develop knowledge and skills in that area.

Community-Based Education Concepts, Skills, Components

The community-based education curriculum for the CMTI incorporates
the following concepts, skills, and components related to that content
area:

Concepts

Community-Based Education
Representativeness
Leadership
Shared Governance/Collaborative Decision-Making
Life-long Learning
Change (change process)
Community

Skills

Decision-Making
Problem Solving
Planning
Programming
Coordinating
Managing
Communicating (Individual/Group)
Assessing/Monitoring/Evaluating
Resolving Conflict

Components of Community-Based Education

The K-12 Curriculum
The Extended Day
Interagency Cooperation
Volunteers and Other Community Resources
Human Service Delivery
Facility Use
Human Resource Development
Parent Education
The Community Council

Operational Definitions of Community-Based Education Concepts

REPRESENTATIVENESS is the insuring that each segment or sub-community

within the broader community to be served is clearly

identified and, through an appropriate selection/election

process, a representative from each sub-community is

included in the formal decision-making structure.

LEADERSHIP is the exercise of processes, authority, or procedures

which move a group or organization toward the achievement

of desired outcomes. CMTI emphasis in this area will focus

on both appropriate and inappropriate leadership roles for

Interns.

SHARED GOVERNANCE/COLLABORATIVE DECISION-MAKING is the process through

which representatives from identified sub-communities are

directly involved in the formal decision-making structure

at all levels.

LIFE-LONG LEARNING is education which is viewed as a continuing process

guided by the overriding goal of improving the quality of

life for all persons, regardless of their age. That involves

commitment to and provision of learning experiences for all

persons in a community.

PLANNED CHANGE   is the systematic implementation of plans designed
(CHANGE PROCESS)
                  to move an organization from one point to another

                  more desirable point. CMTI emphasis will be on

                  the development of systematic planning skills, and

                  on appropriate and inappropriate change efforts

                  and roles for Interns.

COMMUNITY refers to a group of people who share common interests,

                  concerns, or needs and who together engage in such

                  social processes and relationships as may normally

                  arise in the pursuit of the chief concerns of life.

COMMUNITY-BASED EDUCATION is a philosophical concept which promotes the

                  building of collaborative relationships for the

                  purpose of bringing community resources to bear on

                  identified community needs, problems, and concerns

                  through a process of direct community involvement

                  in providing services and programs to enhance the

                  quality of life in the community.

Community-Based Education Objectives

Knowledge Objectives - Week 1

1. Participants will:

    a. Define and Provide a rationale for Community-Based Education.

    b. Describe the basic Community-Based Education components:

        1) the K-12 curriculum
        2) extended day
        3) interagency cooperation
        4) human service delivery
        5) facility use
        6) volunteers and other community resources

       7) parent education
       8) human resource development
       9) community council

2. Participants will describe Teacher Corps requirements as related to Community-Based Education.

Practice Objectives - Week 2

3. Participants will define the following concepts and give examples of the concepts as they are related to Community-Based Education:

a. representativeness
b. leadership
c. shared governance/collaborative decision-making
d. life-long learning
e. change (change process)
f. community

In role-playing or simulation exercises, participants will **demonstrate** leadership skills in:

a. collaborative decision-making
b. resource identification and use
c. interpersonal communications
d. conflict resolution
e. change processes
f. group processes

Application Objective - Week 3

In simulated and local project site-specific problem situations, participants will **apply** planning and problem-solving skills, including:

a. assessing and discrepancy analysis, including:
   1) observing
   2) interviewing
   3) surveying
   4) data analysis
b. goal setting and prioritizing
c. constraint identification and resolution
d. resource identification and use
e. objective setting
f. designing task/activity plans
g. designing assessment and monitoring plans

CMTI INSTRUCTIONAL OBSERVATION SCHEDULE

WK [1] DATE [1 | 8] CLSTR. [0 | 3] OBSR. [5] OBSN. NO. [0 | 1]

1   2   3   4   5   6   7   8

Concept	Observation Segment										Seg. Total		Sum of atnd. rating		
	1	2	3	4	5	6	7	8	9	10					
ORGANIZATION															
Present-low cog.	3	3	2								0 | 3	9-10	0 | 8	43-44
Present-high cog.											0 | 0	11-12	0 | 0	45-46
Discussion-cog.							4				0 | 1	13-14	0 | 4	47-48
Experiential-cog.							5	5	4		0 | 3	15-16	1 | 4	49-50
MULTICULTURE															
Present-low cog.											0 | 0	17-18	0 | 0	51-52
Present-high cog.	3										0 | 1	19-20	0 | 3	53-54
Discussion-cog.				4	4						0 | 2	21-22	0 | 8	55-56
Experiential-cog.							5	5	5	4	0 | 4	23-24	1 | 9	57-58
COMMUNITY															
Present-low cog.											0 | 0	25-26	C | 0	59-60
Present-high cog.											0 | 0	27-28	0 | 0	61-62
Discussion-cog.				4	4	5	5				0 | 4	29-30	1 | 8	63-64
Experiential-cog.											0 | 0	31-32	C | 0	65-66
Experiential-non-cog.											C | 0	33-34	C | 0	67-68
Non-instructional											0 | 0	35-36	C | C	69-70
Total no. segments											1 | 8	37-38	↓	
Sum attend. ratings												→	0 | 7 | 4	71-73

_____ Obsr. ck.   No. learners [3 \| 9] 39-40

_____ Office ck.   No. seg. obs. [1 \| 0] 41-42

Other (code/describe) [| | | | | | | | | |]

(b) For each substantive strand, determine the method of instruction being used. The four choices are presentation of content at lower cognitive levels, presentation of content at higher cognitive levels, discussion, and experiential activities.

Two areas are not related to the three content areas --
(1) experiences that are non-cognitive (generally affective) and
(2) non-instructional experiences

A final row is reserved for experiences that cannot be classified in any of the above categories (Other). Code these 2-minute segments with a letter (a, b, c, etc.), then in the blank space at the bottom of the page, write the alphabetic code and describe the content and processes used.

(c) Determine the extensiveness of attending behavior and rate the appropriate cell using the 1-5 scale described below.

Scale
5. 80% - 100% of participants involved and attending
4. 60% - 79%   "   "   "   "   "
3. 40% - 59%   "   "   "   "   "
2. 20% - 39%   "   "   "   "   "
1   0% - 19%   "   "   "   "   "

Other ways of conceptualizing the scale:

Scale	% Range	Mid-point	Approx. Fractions	When N = 40 Range	Mid.
5	80 - 100%	90%	9/10	32-40	36
4	60 - 79%	70%	2/3	24-31	28
3	40 - 59%	50%	1/2	16-23	20
2	20 - 39%	30%	1/3	8-15	12
1	0 - 19%	10%	1/10	0-7	4

Definitions of Areas

1. Presentation of content at lower cognitive levels. Instruction may use lecture, audio-visual, demonstration, or other methods but is primarily expository and concerned with direct instruction related to multiculture, community, or organization. Typically, the instructors will be primarily responsible, however, participants could be giving information or instructing. Learners may occasionally ask questions, but these primarily are clarifying questions seeking clarifying answers. The level of cognition is either knowledge or comprehension when defined using Bloom's Taxonomy.

2. Presentation of content at higher cognitive levels. The same rules as above apply except that cognitive levels are higher, involving analysis, synthesis, application, or evaluation.

3. Discussion. Learners are engaged in discussion of substantive issues related to multiculture, community, or organization. Participants may be in several groups in room. Students and

instructors discuss their knowledge, experiences, and feelings. Interaction is open.

4. <u>Experiential-cognitive process</u>. Simulations, intellectual games, and role playing are illustrations of experiential activities. The emphasis is on <u>experiencing</u> rather than <u>talking about</u> (discussion). In this factor, the experience must clearly relate either to increased understanding or appreciation of organizational concepts, community concepts, or multicultural education or the relationship is strongly inferred.

5. <u>Experiential non-cognitive process</u>. This includes experiences where the objectives are not related to increasing understanding of organization, multiculture, or community. Activities include get-acquainted exercises, self-development role playing, non-cognitive physical activities designed for group building.

6. <u>Non-instructional activities</u>. This includes periods of transition between activities, breaks for lunch or coffee/juice, administrative tasks, housekeeping activities, and announcements. Their general purpose is maintenance of the organization or periods of confusion.

7. <u>Other</u>. There may be occasions when content is presented that is not related to the three CMTI concepts. Other instances may not be able to be clearly coded. This factor provides an opportunity to code these activities. Since this will not be included in the analysis, it should be used sparingly.

<u>Sequence of Observation Activities</u>

<u>Before an Observation</u>

     a. Complete identification data at top of Observation Schedule (boxes 1-8)
     b. Set stop watch at zero.

<u>During an Observation</u>

     a. Start the stop watch at the time assigned to begin the observation.
     b. During each two-minute segment, rate on 1-5 attending scale all items that are observed (it is not necessary to rate an item more than once in the two-minute segment).
     c. If none of the items are appropriate, code them "Other". Use alphabetic letters as codes, then in the blank space at the bottom of the observation schedule, list each code and describe the event beside the code.
     d. Continue for 20-minutes (ten segments observed). Because observation times are assigned at random, a cluster may break for lunch or free time during the observation period.

e. At the end of the 20-minute period, count the
    number of learners in the observation and record in
    boxes 39-40.
f. Then write a brief description of what happened
    (content, processes, and interesting vignettes)
    on the back of the observation sheet.

After the Observation

a. Count the number of cells with a rating in them
    in each row and record these numbers in the "Seg. Total"
    column (boxes 9-36). These segment totals will range
    from 0-10.
b. Add the number of these segment totals and record
    the grand total in boxes 37-38.
c. Count the number of cells with a rating in them in
    each of the ten columns. Write these sums in the
    shaded area marked "Total no. segments".
d. Add these totals; they should equal the sum in
    boxes 37-38. If not, recheck figures.
e. The same process is completed for the actual ratings.
    First, add the values of ratings in each row and
    write these sums in boxes 43-70.
f. Second, add these sums to find a total for them and
    record this in boxes 71-72.
g. Third, add the ratings in each of the ten columns,
    and write these sums in the shaded area marked
    "Sum attend. ratings".
h. Fourth, add the sums in this "Sum attend. ratings"
    row; this total should equal the figures in boxes
    71-72.
i. Count the number of two-minute segments observed and
    record in boxes 41-42. Unless the observation period
    is shortened, this will be 10. Please try to have
    10 segments for each cluster.
j. Examine each observation schedule to ensure that it
    is accurately and completely filled out. Reread the
    brief description on the back and add any details that
    are missing. Then initial the space marked "Obsr. ck."
    and turn into the office. All observation schedules
    are to be turned in at the end of each day.

An illustration of an observation form that has been completed is
found on the next page. Please note the use of zero for blanks in
key punched boxes.

Recording When More Than One Cluster is Involved

On several occasions, all clusters will attend a general
assembly. A single observation schedule will be completed during
these periods, with all cluster numbers recorded beside boxes 4-5.
When two clusters are involved in the same activity when observed,

record one of their cluster numbers in boxes 4-5 and the other above boxes 4-5.

Balance of Observations

For the most effective analysis of data, each observer must observe each cluster an equal number of times. If you missed a cluster for any reason, please try to pick it up the following day. Further, if all observations were of ten segments each, it would help.

Appendix C

OBSERVER GUIDE

CMTI INSTRUCTIONAL OBSERVATION SCHEDULE

Schedule of Observations

Each cluster will be observed three times on Monday through Friday of each week. Each observation will be 20 minutes. Observation times will be drawn randomly and assigned to observers. Each observer will observe each cluster each day to eliminate any differences attributable to observers.

Identification Data

WK   1 = First Week;   2 = Second Week;   3 = Third Week

DATE   Date of Month

CLSTR.   Record cluster number assigned in CMTI (1-10)

Cluster	Cluster Leader, Instructors
01	Marcia Galli, Don Tobias, Johnnie Mills
02	Carlos Olivarez, Donna Schoeny, Ron Tyrell
03	Jack Croghan, Anna Perez, Taylor Griffin
04	Tony Archuleta, Lauren Young, Marie Nock
05	Daisy Reed, Pat Rice, Gary Watabayashi
06	Wallace Woodard, Guy Chapman, Adelia Morales
07	Mike Barry, Edith Miller, Larry Holiday
08	Brenda Bryant, Juan Garcia, Harlan London
09	Julia Roberts, Jennie Green, Ed Mc Clelland
10	Bill Moore, Brenda Murphy, Tom Konno

OBSR.   Record your assigned observer number
1   Dick Andrews
2   Norma French
3   Cynthia Rodriquez
4   Ted Andrews

OBSN. NO.   Number consecutively your observations, beginning with 01, 02, throughout CMTI

Observations

Observations relate to three areas: (a) the content being presented, (b) the method of instruction, and (c) the proportion of participants "attending" to the instruction.

(a) The major substantive strands in CMTI are Organization, Multiculture, and Community. First, decide if one of these three areas is presented, discussed, or experienced during a 2-minute period.

DIRECTIONS FOR CHECKING OBSERVATION FORMS

A. Observers will turn all forms into the office at the end of each
    day. If there is a problem, discuss it with the observer.

    As observers turn their observation sheets in, (1) quickly look
    over each one for completeness, then (2) record on the Master
    Observation Schedule the total number of observations made by
    the observer that day, and (3) tally these observations by cluster
    on the Master Observation Schedule. If more than one cluster
    is together when an observation is made, tally all clusters and
    be sure all cluster numbers are recorded on or around boxes 4
    and 5 on the CMTI Instructional Observation Schedule.

    When all observers have turned in observation forms for a day,
    write the total in the center column of the Master Observation
    Schedule. This number should equal the sum for observers and
    also the total number of tallies for clusters.

    File forms in "Unchecked Observation Forms" folder.

B. To check each observation Sheet:

    (1) Check to ensure all identification data completed (1-8).

    (2a) Count the number of ratings in each row to ensure they sum
         to the number recorded in the "Seg. total" column (boxes
         9-10 through 35-36).

    (2b) Add the "Seg. totals" column to be sure it agrees with
         total in boxes 37-38.

    (2c) Add column totals in "total no. segments" to be sure it
         agrees with total in boxes 37-38. This gives a double
         check on accuracy of data in 37-38.

    (3a) Add the values of ratings in each row to check them against
         those in the "Sum of Atnd. rating" column.

    (3b) Add the "Sum of Atnd. rating" column to ensure it totals
         to boxes in 71-72.

    (3c) Add column totals in "Sum Atnd. ratings to be sure it
         agrees with total in 71-72.

    (4) No. Learners recorded (39-40).

    (5) No. Segments recorded in 41-42 agrees with no. columns
        observed (typically this would be 10).

    (6) Any "Other" behaviors coded and described (process and con-
        tent) at bottom of page.

    (7) On back of page, description of experience or vignette
        written.

(8) Initials of observer recorded.

C. After examining forms, initial each to indicate you have
completed the analysis, then file them in the "Checked Observation Forms" folder.

D. Maintaining balance among observers and clusters is important.
The perfect system would have
(1) all observations have 10 segments completed.
(2) all clusters are observed each day by each observer.
If observers can complete the ten segments, even if they must
return at a later time to do so, this would make the system more
effective.

We must ensure that clusters are observed an equal number of times;
thus, check this each day and on Fridays. Sunday evenings at
general assemblies is a good time to increase the number of observations per cluster, and to "make up" for missed observations
by cluster or by observer. Our goal is 45 observations per cluster
(14 days x 3 plus 3 general assemblies).